W9-CFQ-147

HOOKED RUGS

HOOKED RUGS

ANN DAVIES AND EMMA TENNANT

Sterling Publishing Co., Inc. New York
A STERLING/MUSEUM QUILTS BOOK

Editors: Ljiljana Baird and Eleanor Van Zandt
Designer: Yvonne Dedman
Typesetter: Claire Benge
Photographer: Steve Tanner (pages 2, 14, 24)

Library of Congress Cataloging-in-Publication Data available

2 4 6 8 10 9 7 5 3 1

A STERLING/MUSEUM QUILTS BOOK

Published by Sterling Publishing Company, Inc.,
387 Park Avenue South, New York, NY 10016
and by Museum Quilts Publications Inc.
Published in the UK by Museum Quilts (UK) Inc.,
254–258 Goswell Road, London EC1V 7EB
Distributed in Canada by Sterling Publishing
c/o Canadian Manda Group, One Atlantic Avenue, Suite 105
Toronto, Ontario, Canada M6K 3E7
Distributed in Australia by Capricorn Link (Australia) Pty Ltd.,
P.O. Box 6651, Baulkham Hills Business Centre
NSW 2153, Australia

Copyright © Museum Quilts Publications, Inc., 1995

Color illustrations © Penny Brown 1995
Line illustrations © Anny Evason 1995

All rights reserved.
No part of this publication may be reproduced or transmitted in any form
or by any means, electronic or mechanical, including photocopy, recording,
or any information storage and retrieval system now known or to be invented
without permission in writing from the publishers.

The authors have endeavored to ensure that all project instructions are accurate.
However, due to variations in readers' individual skill and materials available,
neither the authors nor the publishers can accept responsibility for damages or
losses resulting from the instructions herein. All instructions should be studied
and clearly understood before beginning any project.

Printed & bound by ORIENTAL PRESS, (DUBAI).
ISBN 0-8069-1338-X Trade
ISBN 0-8069-1339-8 Paper

CONTENTS

❖

Society for the Preservation of New England Antiquities, Boston; Cogswell's Grant, Essex, Massachusetts; Gift of Bertram K. and Nina Fletcher Little. Photograph by David Bohl.

INTRODUCTION

❖

EMMA TENNANT

The craft of making rugs from rags is a very old one. Until recently, however, it has been unjustly neglected—outside North America. While exotic textiles such as Indonesian batik and Middle Eastern felt-work have been collected, studied, and written about, the humble rag rug has been almost forgotten in Great Britain, its country of origin. Too lowly to figure in written records, and not rated highly enough to be handed down as family heirlooms, old "hookies" and "clippies" were usually thrown away. As a result, it is very difficult to trace their history accurately or to make firm claims about the origin of the various techniques used in making them.

Glowing shades of red enliven the basket of flowers in this hooked rug, made in New England between 1880 and 1900. The design is worked in strips of wool on a burlap ground (39 x 37¼ inches).

The Scottish embroiderer Ann Macbeth, who was the influential head of the needlework department at the Glasgow School of Art before the First World War, became very interested in rag rugs when, in the 1920s, she went to live at Patterdale in the Lake District. There, nearly every cottage and farmhouse was complete with homemade rugs, both upstairs in the bedrooms and downstairs in the living room and kitchen. Miss Macbeth's research suggested the possibility of links with the culture of the Vikings, who had settled in the area so long ago. She pointed out that their influence was apparent in the place names and dialect words, as well as in design. Some of the curves and scrolls that figure in traditional rugs may have been copied from carved furniture whose decoration resembled Scandinavian design. There were similarities in technique, too. "Rye" or "rya" rugs, made by pulling loops of wool through a woven backing, were mentioned in Scandinavian inventories and wills in about 1700, and fragments of clothes made in the same very primitive way have been found in Danish Bronze Age graves. The word "rya" may be related to the Anglo-Saxon *ryhe*, meaning "torn cloth." The link between the Scandinavian tradition and Britain could well have been Orkney and Shetland, Norse islands which became part of Scotland under the marriage settlement of James III in the fifteenth century. For hundreds of years hooked rugs, made by "rug women" who traveled from island to island, were part of every Orcadian bride's dowry. Like the earliest American rugs, they were used to warm the bed rather than the floor. The tradition has died out only within the last hundred years. Whether or not Miss Macbeth's conjectures are right, it is certainly true, as she pointed out, that though rag rugs were made all over the British Isles, from the west of Ireland to East Anglia, and from Land's End to John O'Groats, the tradition was the strongest in the ancient kingdom of Strathclyde, from north Lanarkshire down to Morecambe Bay, in Lancashire.

Ann Macbeth corresponded with the American architect and historian William Winthrop Kent, whose book *The Hooked Rug*, published in New York in 1937, remains a classic. He shows two eighteenth-century hooked bed rugs, one dated 1763 and the other 1773. Both have a sophisticated design of twining stems adorned with flowers, fruit, and leaves, and must have been drawn by an artist familiar with the contemporary crewel work and chintz. Another early hearth rug was dated 1830, and it, too, shows a far-from-primitive floral border surrounding a symmetrical basket of flowers, with two birds completing the design.

These examples are unusually sophisticated and in marked contrast to most of the American rugs made before 1850. They were usually humble artifacts, designed at home by men and women who took their subject matter from their surroundings and depicted it with childlike simplicity. Life in those days was hard, with long, cold winters and no luxuries. Bought textiles were extremely expensive, so the thrifty American housewife depended on wool or linen that was spun, woven, and dyed at home. Nothing was wasted. Every little scrap and the least worn parts of old clothes went into the ragbag to be re-used; the cotton for patchwork quilts, and the woolen for rag rugs.

Life in the country and small towns, where most people then lived, revolved around animals and crops. Dogs, cats—the traditional guardians of the hearth—horses, cattle, and poultry were favorite subjects. Beavers were popular in Canada, and an exotic lion, perhaps seen at a traveling circus or inspired by one of Bewick's wood engravings from his *History of Quadrupeds* (1790), sometimes appears. The seafaring communities on the coast had their own favorite motifs. Schooners in full sail, open fishing boats, lighthouses, whales, anchors, ropes, shells, and mermaids are depicted against swirly backgrounds which suggest the movement of sea and sky.

Flowers, fruit, and leaves, worked in bright colors, cheered up the living room through the long, dark winters. Sometimes the house itself was depicted, complete with picket fence and garden trees, or even the owner's favorite horse. Abstract designs often used the familiar vocabulary of patchwork quilts. Such patterns as "log cabin," "baby's blocks," and "clamshell," with its overlapping circles drawn around cups or saucers, were very effective when the maker had a good eye for color.

The "crazy quilt" or "broken glass" pattern was another good way of using up small amounts of different colors. The simplest of all abstract designs, also found in both America and Britain, consists of a border of black or another dark color enclosing a field worked in straight or wavy lines in a random mixture of colors. It is called "hit or miss" in America, "scrappie" in Canada, and "mixy," "mizzy-mazzy," or "hundreds and thousands" in England. Very often a central diamond or lozenge in a contrasting plain color, is included.

Dyeing is a craft that has always gone hand-in-hand with rug making. Before the middle of the nineteenth century homemade vegetable dyes provided a wide range of colors. Reseda, hemlock bark, yellow hickory, peach leaves, walnut skins, goldenrod, sumac, blueberries, sassafras, and onion skins were some of the most useful. Synthetic dyes, which were available from the 1860s, produced brighter but harsher colors.

The first commercially printed rug patterns were produced by a firm in Massachusetts at about the same time. But the best-known designs were the work of

This American townscape, dating from the mid-1800s, is hooked in wool on a linen backing fabric (35 x 70½ inches).

"Frost the Rugman." Edward Sands Frost was invalided out of the U.S. army in 1863. He earned his living as a peddler of tinware in Maine. One day his wife started to make a rag rug. An artistic cousin drew it for her; then she attached it to her quilting frame and started to work with a hook made from an old nail. Frost, a one-time mechanic, began by making her a better hook. Then he thought he could improve on the design his wife was working. Neighbors admired his pattern of flowers and scrolls, and he was soon busy sketching on burlap (known as hessian in Britain) with orders coming in faster than he could fill them. The next breakthrough came when he began to stencil the designs—thus reducing ten hours' work to two and a half hours—and finally he developed a method of printing them in color. A real American success story, Frost died a rich man in 1894, and his designs continued to be sold by mail order after his death.

Most of the Sands designs used the traditional hooked rug motifs. An oval centerpiece, which may be floral, or show a lion, a horse, a Dalmatian or a bird on its nest, is usually surrounded by a border of scrolls or ropes or leaves. His catalog of nearly 200 designs also included copies of oriental carpets.

The Currier Gallery of Art, Manchester, New Hampshire; Currier Fund, 1932.

Society for the Preservation of New England Antiquities, Boston; Cogswell's Grant, Essex, Massachusetts; Gift of Bertram K. and Nina Fletcher Little. Photograph by David Bohl.

Animals have been popular subjects for hooked rugs since the beginnings of the craft. A fine example is this design featuring a stag and hunting dog from late-nineteenth-century New England (67 x 76 inches).

Miss Macbeth would not have approved. In 1927 she wrote to William Winthrop Kent, "I do not believe in copying old examples. One is always influenced by them to some extent, but as soon as the individual stops inventing and relies on manufacturers' patterns the craft dies, all that is best in it at least, and my whole working aim is to stir up inventiveness, it matters not in what material or craft, for I feel we have lost touch with the holy spirit [*sic*], because we have left too much to the machines." In England, as in America, printed designs had appeared by the time she wrote this. Although they stifled originality, these designs are of interest, being themselves part of the history of taste. The stylized flowers of the 1920s and '30s, with their hints of Art Deco, are typical of their time.

By this time, in the United States, rag rugs had developed from a humble craft into a valued art form, with collectors paying hundreds of dollars for good examples. By contrast, in Britain the hooked rug remained firmly in its place—in front of the fire in the farmhouse or miner's cottage.

The oldest dated English rug that I have traced was made in 1851, though I have heard of one made in 1815 from army uniforms worn in the Napoleonic wars. The scarcity of old rugs in England is not surprising. It was the custom in many places to make a new rug every winter. As soon as the harvest was in and the dark evenings arrived, the whole family settled down to work. The man of the house, who had usually made the frame and hook himself, often drew the design on the backing with a charred stick. The backing was usually a burlap sack, opened out and washed. Sacks used for animal food or grain were sometimes printed with a bold trademark, such as a rooster or a cornstalk, which was an ideal ready-made design. These sacks were eagerly sought after by rug makers. If burlap was not available, sugar or hop sacks were sometimes used, and if all else failed, it was possible to knit a suitable backing. During the Second World War, with England's Home Front slogan of "Make Do and Mend," washed sand-bags were sometimes used.

Rug making was a very sociable activity. The children helped cut up the scraps and old clothes, which had been saved over the past few months. Their parents, along with friends and neighbors who dropped in to help, worked away at the frame, which was big enough to accommodate several people at once. Rag rugs were part of life in the country and in the industrial towns of northern England—as necessary on the cold stone floor of a miner's row house as on the beaten earth of a farmworker's cottage. A neighbor of mine, an old Scottish lady, remembers the custom well: "The word would go round the village, so-and-so is putting up a pair of stenters [the Scottish word for a frame]. Then we would all go and give a hand." Children on their way home from school did a few minutes' work on their neighbor's rug and were rewarded with a piece of homemade toffee.

There was a great celebration when the new rug was finished. It was laid down in front of the fire in the best room, and the youngest child in the family rolled on it—though the dog or cat often got there first. Some families put the new rug down as soon as the house had been spring-cleaned, which was a big event in those days. Others had a tradition of using it for the first time at Christmas. The old hearth rug would be moved to the kitchen, that one became a doormat, and the dirty old doormat went outside, either to the dog-kennel or to cover the potatoes or the pile of firewood. Eventually it was thrown away. This three or four-year rotation is the reason why relatively few old rugs survive.

Among those that do, there are some fascinating examples, though one must admit that the majority of British rugs are dull beside their American cousins. Abstract designs include the familiar diamond on a "mixy" background; concentric lines of drab color surrounding a brighter centerpiece; a geometric diagonal

Rug making was a social activity, and often involved all members of the family.

North of England Open Air Museum: Beamish, Co. Durham.

Photograph by Ken Taylor

A traditional rug pattern of an animal skin with a "tail" at each end of the oval body. Made by Mrs. F. Scott in the mid-twentieth century in Cumberland, England (30½ x 51¼ inches).

pattern based on the St. Andrew's cross or, more elaborate, the Union Jack. As in America, many of the designs are taken from patchwork.

County Durham was famous for its quilts, and quilting patterns, often based on shells, scrolls, or feathers, were used for rag rugs too. The templates were cut out of stiff paper and kept to be handed down to the next generation. A popular Cumberland pattern, featuring a curvy central lozenge, is said to have been based on a simplified representation of the oldest rug of all—an animal skin thrown down on the floor. It has a "tail" at each end of the oval "body"—probably because the head was too difficult to draw, and would have been asymmetrical—and four stylized paws. Borders were decorated with scallops drawn around cups or saucepan lids, which were also used as templates for simple

flower designs. A rug in the collection at Beamish Open Air Museum, County Durham, celebrates Queen Victoria's Jubilee. It includes the date, 1897, a central crown, and the words "DIAMOND JUBILEE" in bright red against a "mixy" background. One very sophisticated rug in the same museum was made by a Mrs. Latymer in 1904. A wide floral border encloses a panel of interlaced sprays of flowers and leaves in shades of red and yellow. Who was Mrs. Latymer, and where did she get the idea for her beautiful rug? Perhaps she worked in a big house and was familiar with Aubusson or Savonnerie carpets.

The rug maker's palette was limited by what was available in the way of woolen material. Most old clothes came in somber shades of black, gray, brown, or dark blue. Then as now, the broken color of checked or herringbone tweed was especially effective. The scarlet of a man's hunting coat was highly coveted in country districts. In mill towns "clippings" of cloth could be bought cheaply, and old red uniforms were sometimes sold by sergeants at army barracks, enabling rug makers to outline their designs with a *real* "thin red line." Navy uniforms were used if available; in Dorset and Hampshire rag rugs were known as "soldiers' coats and sailors' trousers."

In Cumberland there was a tradition of depicting animals on rugs. Such a one caught the attention of the painters Ben and Winifred Nicholson in 1923 when, soon after their marriage, they moved into a new farmhouse (set into Hadrian's Wall) near Brampton, East Cumberland. The Nicholsons' next-door neighbor was a farmer's wife named Margaret Warwick, who designed her own rugs. She made one for Ben and Winifred. It depicted two black cats sitting by a glowing fire. The traditional black border was enlivened by black and red rosettes. Intrigued by the technique, Ben designed a larger rug, which was made by Mrs. Warwick's daughter Mary. It had a checkerboard pattern. The plain squares were worked in Ben's favorite neutral colors, except for the central one, which was made from red plaid. The animal squares showed portraits of a brown horse, a Border collie, a turkey, a cat, a rooster, a ram, a black hen, and a white duck. As the Nicholsons' son Jake has pointed out, "It did not look out of place with the abstract painting by Piet Mondrian which hung on the wall."

Winifred Nicholson had grown up nearby, and was a true countrywoman, with a deep interest in local traditions, as well as being an extremely accomplished artist. She was thus the ideal person to encourage a revival of rug making. She took the idea up again many years later, in the 1960s. The tradition was still alive in East Cumberland, but most people bought ready-printed burlap, whose banal designs horrified Winifred. Idealist that she was, she believed that her neighbors were capable of drawing much more interesting rugs themselves. She and her son Jake started a company called Foursquare Designs, which sold nearly 200 rugs. Two of the company's most talented designers were Margaret Warwick's daughters Mary Berrids and Janet Heap; their rugs usually depicted farm animals.

My own early efforts were inspired both by some interesting old American rugs in the collection of a friend and by the examples I saw when I visited Mrs. Nicholson to see her paintings. Before that I had not been aware of the possibility of making sophisticated pictorial designs in such a simple medium. Nor has the tradition died out in the Nicholson family. Louisa Creed, Winifred's niece, makes delightful rugs, including portraits of their cats. She is a professional musician who finds rug making a good way of relaxing.

There is no doubt that a revival of rag rug making is underway in Britain. For a long time the craft was underrated, probably because it was associated with poverty and the hard times of "Make Do and Mend." Rag rugs were children of necessity, made by families who could not afford to buy a warm and attractive floor covering. Now they are made as a creative and relaxing hobby by women who have more leisure than their ancestors ever dreamed of. This new approach means that a whole new vocabulary of design is being developed. I take my ideas from my surroundings: the Scottish landscape, the changing weather, the animals on the farm, and the flowers and fruit in the garden. I need look no farther than the kitchen dresser or a vase on the window sill. One of the things I enjoy most about designing and making rugs is the way that it has opened my eyes and sharpened my perception of a thousand and one details of my surroundings that I never noticed before. As John Ruskin said, "Design is not the offspring of idle fancy. It is the studied result of accumulative observation and delightful habit."

"Gate and Green Corn" by Emma Tennant.

MAKING HOOKED RUGS

❖

ANN DAVIES

After a long period of time in the doldrums, the craft of rug hooking is now enjoying a spirited revival. There is a growing awareness of the satisfaction that can be gained from this craft and of the infinite variety of designs and materials that can be used for it. Perhaps this is because we are now more environmentally aware and conscious of how much material we have been wasting. Also, as fabrics and yarns for other textile crafts become so expensive, we see that besides being satisfying, rag rug making is a craft that need not incur great expense.

Of the various ways of making rag rugs—hooking strips to the right side, prodding the fabric through from the wrong side, and braiding strips which are then sewn together—hooking is easily the most popular, and this is the technique featured in this book. It can be used not only for rugs but also for wallhangings, cushion covers, and a variety of other useful articles.

❖ EQUIPMENT ❖

Only a few items of equipment are needed for rug hooking; the hook itself, a frame, and scissors are the basics, but you will need a few other items too .

Hooks In the United States and Canada, where the craft is most widely practiced, hooks come in a range of sizes intended for different widths of strip, from No.1, the smallest, to No.10, the largest. American hooks are shaped like a crochet hook.

In the rest of the world the range is more limited. I use just one hook (see fig. 1), which, because the shank is shaped and it has a very acute point, can be used for a great range of strip widths.

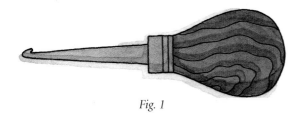

Fig. 1

Frames Some kind of frame is essential. It holds the backing fabric taut, freeing both hands for the work and helping you to keep the loops even. To begin with, you can use a simple frame made of artist's stretchers. These are four pieces of wood that slot together at the corners. They are available in various sizes from art supply stores. Bear in mind, however, that the maximum size you can use is about 28 inches, as you have to be able to reach comfortably into the center of the frame. The work can be moved on the frame, by removing the thumbtacks from the backing fabric edges and carefully re-inserting them through a worked area.

Many rug hookers like to use a quilting hoop—some of which are equipped with a stand. Make sure, though, that the screw that adjusts the outer hoop is long enough to allow for the additional thickness of the completed hooking. Also, make it a practice to remove the hoop when you finish a section to avoid crushing the loops.

When using a stretcher frame or a hoop without a stand, you may find it easier to lean it against a table than to hold it on your lap.

In North America there are various frames, portable and otherwise, designed specifically for rug hooking. Elsewhere the choice is far more limited. There are some excellent handmade frames for making rugs, but because they are handcrafted, they tend to be expensive. Some of these are similar to an embroiderer's scroll

Some of the materials and equipment required for making hooked rugs, including burlap, fabrics for the strips, the hook, dressmaking shears, napping scissors, a cutting board, a stretcher frame, rug-binding tape, and strong sewing thread.

frame, and in fact a scroll frame can be used for rugs—provided that it is strong enough. The cheaper models are too fragile to cope with the weight and tension entailed in rug hooking.

Whatever kind of frame you are using, always try to sit comfortably in a straight-backed chair in a well-lit area.

Scissors Good-quality dressmaking shears or electric scissors are required for cutting the fabrics (do not use them for paper, which dulls the blades). A pair of napping scissors, though not essential, is useful for cutting strip ends close to the pile. They can also be used to shear the loops for a velvet-effect pile.

To simplify the work, you can buy a special strip-cutting machine (see fig. 2), which cuts several strips at a time to a chosen width, governed by a selection of different heads.

Another alternative is to use a rotary cutter and self-healing plastic mat, along with a plastic ruler designed for use with the mat; these items are available from stores selling patchwork supplies. The mats are surprisingly expensive, but they last a long time.

For attaching the rug binding you will need a large tapestry needle or carpet needle and strong thread such as linen or carpet thread, as well as a thimble to make the job easier on your hands.

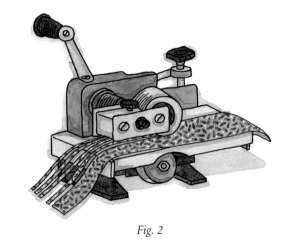

Fig. 2

For transferring designs you may need (depending on the method you are using) sheets of graph paper and tracing paper (large ones are available from art supply stores), a transfer pencil, a felt-tip marker, masking tape, card for cutting templates, a compass, a set square and a ruler.

A sewing machine is useful for stitching around the edges of the backing, but not essential.

❖ MATERIALS ❖

The fabric used for the strips has traditionally been wool. Cotton has also been used, but not so extensively, mainly because it has no natural spring and tends to flatten very easily. The Amish often used cotton, and some of their old rugs now look as flat as a mosaic or a pointillist painting, because the loops have been squashed down by constant wear.

Today many rug hookers continue to use only wool. This is especially true in North America, where manufacturers offer wool fabrics intended specifically for the craft, at good prices. In Britain and other parts of Europe, buying pure new wool for a rug is an expensive proposition. An alternative is to use recycled wool from cast-off garments or old blankets. Thrift shops can be useful sources of recycled clothing, and dressmakers often have wool scraps suitable for rugs.

Today, rug hookers are experimenting with a variety of different fabrics to produce unusual effects. Everything from old sweatshirts and sweaters to velvet, Lurex, denim, ribbons, and vinyl has been used at various times, especially for wallhangings, in which considerations of durability do not apply.

If you intend to use synthetic fabrics, do not attempt to cut the strips on a machine, as the fibers will clog up the workings.

Whatever fabrics you are using—new or recycled—always wash them before hooking. If you are recycling a garment, first take it to pieces, removing buttons, zippers, and such, before washing.

The base material is now usually a good-quality burlap. A 12-ounce burlap, which has about 15 threads to the inch, is most generally useful; 10-ounce burlap has a looser weave; 14-ounce is very fine. Monk's cloth, a soft cotton fabric with a closer weave than burlap, is an alternative, and is preferred by some rug hookers. Another alternative—though a rather expensive one—is linen.

❖ ENLARGING THE DESIGN ❖

Before you can transfer a rug design onto the backing fabric, you need to enlarge it to the required size. There are several methods of doing this.

Enlarging the designs in this book The projects given in these pages are accompanied by diagrams showing the outlines. A grid has been superimposed on each diagram (except in the case of designs already based on a grid) to enable you to scale it up to the correct size. Each square of the grid represents 2 inches on the full-size design.

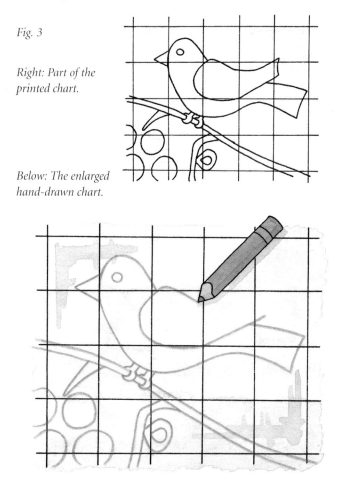

Fig. 3

Right: Part of the printed chart.

Below: The enlarged hand-drawn chart.

If you wish to scale the design up by hand, you can do this either on a large sheet of graph paper or on tracing paper (or, if you are confident of your drawing ability, directly onto the fabric). First draw a grid of 2 inch squares, containing the same number of squares as the printed grid. If you are using graph paper, simply darken the lines every 2 inches. Then copy the design by hand (see fig. 3), positioning the outlines as they appear on the smaller printed grid.

Alternatively, you can take the original design to a copy shop and have it enlarged mechanically to the correct size. However, you may need to do this in sections and then tape the sections together to achieve the size required.

Note that in some cases the diagram has been divided in two across two pages. Where the inner edges are on a grid line, these two lines count as a single line on the enlarged grid; that is, they should be superimposed.

Enlarging designs from other sources Where no grid or finished size is given—or if you wish to determine the size yourself—use the following method.

1. Mark the size of the finished rug on your backing fabric by running a pencil firmly down in the channel between two threads. Cut out a piece of brown wrapping paper (or similar) to the same size. Fold the paper in half lengthwise and then in half widthwise. Then fold it again and again into equal-sized rectangles.

2. On the printed design mark a grid containing the same number of rectangles as on the full-size paper. If you don't wish to mark the original source, draw the grid on tracing paper and place it over the design with masking tape or weights.

3. Copy the design onto the brown paper using the grid as a guide, as in the method illustrated.

❖ **PREPARATION** ❖

Before you begin to hook you will need to sort the fabrics into the different colors and color families for the different parts of the design so that you won't have to hunt through a mass of material to find a particular

shade. I find it useful to keep the various colors in separate clear plastic bags.

1. Cut the backing fabric approximately 3 inches larger than the size of the finished rug. It is best to pull out one of the fabric threads to serve as a guide for cutting. This will help in straightening the edges later. Stitch around the edges with a medium-width zigzag-stitch to prevent fraying. If you haven't got a sewing machine, you can overcast the edges by hand.

2. Transfer the enlarged design to the fabric. (In some cases you may wish to do this after framing up the fabric; see below.) There are several ways of doing this.

◆ One way is by using one of the transfer pens and pencils available. These enable you to make your own transfer pattern—similar to commercial embroidery transfers—which you then iron onto the backing. Place the enlarged design on a flat surface, then place a sheet of tracing paper over it and fix it in place with masking tape at the corners. Trace the design, then turn the tracing over and draw over the design lines using the transfer pen or pencil (see fig. 4).

Fig. 4

Place the tracing, right side up, on the backing and secure it with a few pins. Turn the iron to a high setting and apply it to the paper; place it firmly on one area and allow time for the lines to be transferred, then move it to an adjacent area and repeat. Do not slide it around, as for ironing. It is advisable to practice this method on a scrap piece of material before transferring the design itself.

◆ I have recently discovered a transfer pen that doesn't need a hot iron to transfer the design. You reverse the tracing in the same way but just apply pressure with a fingernail or the rounded end of a teaspoon.

◆ Simple shapes can be cut from cardboard then drawn around on the fabric with a felt-tip marker.

◆ If the design is simple, or if you are sufficiently confident of your drawing ability, you can frame up the fabric then draw the design directly onto it using a felt-tip marker—perhaps marking a grid on the fabric first (see "Enlarging the design" above), thus dispensing with tracings, transfer pencils, and templates.

3. Frame up the fabric. Mounting the fabric in a quilting hoop is quite simple. You separate the rings, place the fabric over the smaller ring and press the larger ring down on top, so that it grips the fabric. You may need to adjust the screw first to make it fit tightly.

To mount fabric on a stretcher frame, use thumbtacks or, if you prefer, a staple gun. First fasten the fabric to the frame along one side, placing the thumbtacks at intervals of about ¾ inch. Then fasten one adjacent edge in the same way, working out from the attached corner, to make an L shape (see fig. 5). This will give you two straight edges, even if the fabric was slightly distorted on the bolt. Now attach the remaining two sides, pulling them taut.

If you are using an adjustable rug frame of the type shown here, make a hem in the two shorter sides, large enough to slip over the doweling, using strong thread and basting (large running) stitches. Slide the doweling through the hems, then slip the fabric-covered doweling into the end pieces (see fig. 6). Roll up one end of the fabric, if necessary, and attach the doweling to the side pieces using the pegs, making sure that it is taut (see fig. 7). When working the design, unroll the fabric as required.

For more elaborate frames, follow the manufacturer's instructions.

4. Cut some strips of fabric for hooking. You will probably need to experiment to determine the best width of

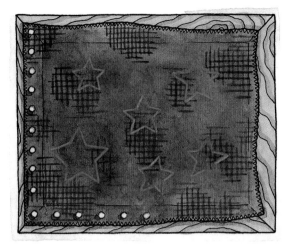

Fig. 5

Fig. 6

Fig. 7

ESTIMATING FABRIC REQUIREMENTS

You can estimate fabric requirements by measurement or by weight.

◆ **To estimate by measurement**, take a single thickness of material and place it over the part of the design you want to cover, so it is completely covered. You will need between four and five thicknesses of fabric to fill that particular area.

◆ **Estimates by weight** are based on the accepted rule that it takes about ½ pound of fabric to fill 1 square foot of backing.

Because some people cut wider than others, or bring their loops up higher, it is better to estimate generously to allow for these variations, whether you are estimating by weight or by measurement.

strip for the design and for your fabrics; thinner fabrics will need to be cut wider than thick ones to produce the same bulk. Test the strips on the chosen backing fabric to gauge the effect. Cut the strips on the straight grain of the fabric; if the fabric can be torn, so much the better.

If you are using a rotary cutter and mat, first straighten one edge of the fabric. Lay this edge along one of the vertical lines on the mat; fold the fabric cross-

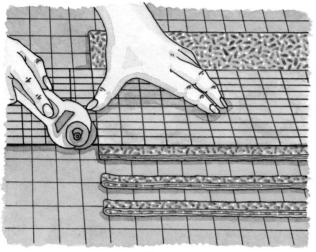

Fig. 8

wise if you are cutting a long strip. Place the ruler the required distance away from the edge. Push the rotary cutter away from you (see fig. 8) in a smooth, firm movement, keeping the blade perpendicular to the mat. (Note: rotary cutters are very sharp. Every time you stop cutting—for even a few moments—slide the safety cover over the blade. This will soon become automatic—and may prevent an accident.)

Strips can be of any length, from about 6 inches upward. You need not cut them all in advance; cut and hook alternately as you like.

❖ HOW TO HOOK ❖

The hooking action itself is very simple. (These instructions and illustrations assume a right-handed person; if you are left-handed, reverse them.)

1. Take a strip of the fabric and, making a loop, hold it in your left hand under the backing material.

2. In your right hand hold the hook as if you were going to write with it, with the hook pointing upward (see fig. 9).

3. Push the hook firmly into the backing and pick up the loop (see fig. 10a), making sure the hook picks up the whole width of the strip. Make a good big hole with the shank of the hook, so that you will be able to draw the point of the hook back up through the fabric without catching it on the threads.

4. Pull the loop up through to the top and continue pulling to draw the loose end through, leaving about 1 inch free; this end will be trimmed level with the loops later (see fig. 10b).

5. Working from right to left and leaving about two threads unworked, again push the hook firmly into the backing material. Hold the strip of fabric in your left hand loosely between your thumb and forefinger. (It must be allowed to run freely—if you hold it tightly you will pull out the strip or loop previously brought up.) Make sure the hook goes right under the strip, and then pull up the strip to the right side of the material, making a loop about ⅜ inch high (see fig. 11).

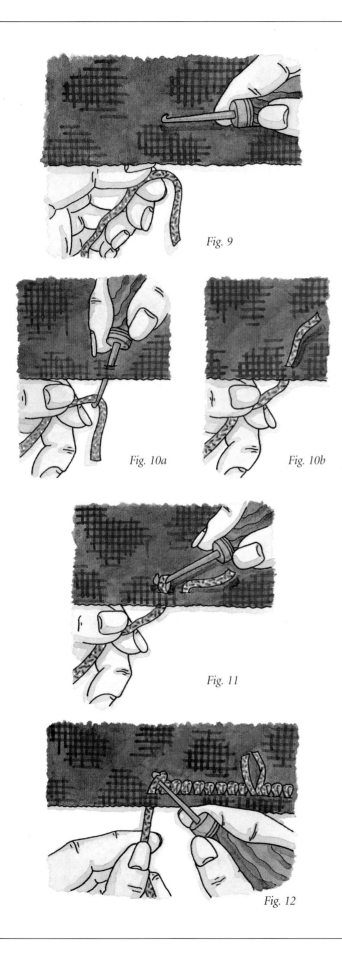

Fig. 9

Fig. 10a   *Fig. 10b*

Fig. 11

Fig. 12

The aim is to have the loops close enough together so that you don't see any of the backing fabric between the loops but not packed so tightly together that it causes the rug to "hump" when taken from the frame. Try to keep the loops at a uniform height (this will vary according to the project).

6. Continue working step 5 until you reach the end of the strip.

7. When you come to the end of the strip, pull the end up to the top. Start the new strip in the same hole in which the last strip ended, thus making sure that you have the same double thickness in that hole as in those containing loops (see fig. 12).

You will know that you are hooking correctly if you have a row of what appears to be closely worked running stitches on the back. If you have any bumps on the back it means you are not making a large enough hole to bring up your loops.

Never be tempted to carry a strip of material across the back from one place to another. If you want to start the same color elsewhere, always bring up a loop, cut off the strip and start again in the new place. Never leave any loose ends on the reverse of the work; bring them to the front and cut them level with the loops.

◆ If your design has strong outlines, work the outlines first.

◆ When beginning a row above or below your first row, leave about two threads between the rows.

◆ Unless you need a straight line, work in curves—the rows meld better.

◆ Some experts advocate starting at a definite point, such as in the center or at the edges. I prefer to use my hook as a paintbrush, putting in material where I wish as the mood takes me. However, if I am hooking a piece of work that has a lot of background in one color, I do some of the pattern and then some of the background and in this way don't have the dreariness of filling in all the background at one time.

The first question often asked by novice rug hookers is "What stops the loops from coming out?" To answer this question, I advise you try a small experiment. Push your hook firmly into the backing and then remove it.

Pulling the strip through, from the wrong side of the rug, to make a loop. From the underside the hooking should look like a smooth row of running stitches.

Here the rug-binding tape is being sewn to the edge of the rug. Note the short end of tape left for finishing later.

You will see that a hole has been made. Then push the hook into the mesh adjacent to the hole and you will see the first hole close up. The pressure of the threads against the loops keeps the loops firmly in place.

Before removing the rug from the frame, check whether there are gaps. These can be seen from the back. If there are, lightly push toothpicks into the gaps so that they show at the front, and hook into the gaps, trying not to pack the loops too tightly. Trim the fabric ends level with the loops.

1. Remove the rug from the frame.

2. Brush lightly over the pile with a firm clothesbrush to remove any fluff, or run a vacuum attachment over it. If you are nervous about the possibility of the loops being drawn up into the vacuum cleaner (many people are, although there is no danger of this), you can cover the vacuum head with a piece of net.

3. Block the rug as follows: place it on a large towel with the pile facing down. Cover the back of the rug with a damp cotton cloth. Press firmly with a hot iron, again using a stamping, not a gliding, motion. Keep the rug flat and allow it to dry.

4. Bind the edges of the rug with rug binding tape. This is a twill-weave cotton tape, available in widths of 1¼–1½ inches and in neutral colors such as cream and tan. If you like, you can dye it to tone with the edge of the rug. In any case, when buying the binding, allow for the fact that it can shrink by up to about 2 inches per yard, and buy extra accordingly. Also allow extra for turning under the raw ends.

Before applying the binding, wash it thoroughly and iron it. (Note: do not be tempted to use adhesive binding tape; a securely sewn-on tape is essential to protect the rug from the wear it will receive.)

Trim the excess backing to about 1 inch all around the rug, trimming diagonally across the corners to reduce bulk.

Using strong thread and beginning halfway along one side, backstitch the binding tape right up to the edge of the hooked area. As you sew around the corners, ease the tape slightly, but don't allow any excess (see fig. 13). Hem all the way around. Turn back the two ends (see fig. 14) and butt them together.

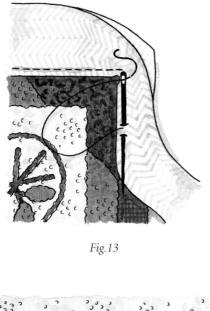

Fig.13

Fig.14

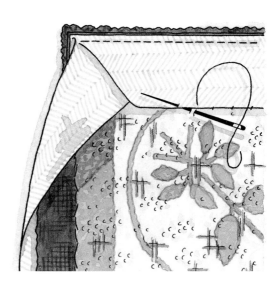

Fig.15

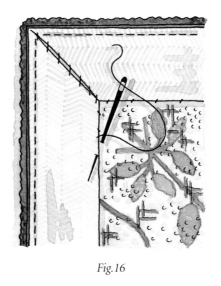

Fig.16

Turn the binding and excess burlap to the wrong side, and hem the binding in place by hand. Miter the corners as shown (see fig. 15) and overcast the diagonal folds together (see fig. 16).

◆ If you are binding an oval or round rug, make small slashes in the excess burlap at intervals of about 2–3 inches, after stitching the binding to the right side. When you turn the binding to the wrong side, the little sections of backing will overlap each other smoothly, preventing a bulky effect. The free edge of the binding will need to be drawn in slightly for a smooth finish. Alternatively, you can make your own binding, cut on the bias of the fabric, which will go around curves more smoothly.

◆ Some people like to back their rugs, but I don't recommend it, for if you do so and grit falls through, the grit can act as an abrasive against the back of your rug and weaken it.

◆ Some modern rug makers use white glue to seal the back of their rugs, and some use it for finishing off the edges, but I do not advocate this method, for two reasons. First, no one knows the long-term effect of white glue on fabrics; secondly, if you have a disaster and your rug is marked or damaged, it is impossible to remove the damaged or stained strips and re-hook.

◆ A useful tip: if you have any spare strips of material left after hooking a project, place some of them between the rug and the binding so that you have some easily accessible strips for repair if necessary.

◆ Always sign (or initial) and date your rugs, either by incorporating this information into your hooking or by sewing a label onto the back of the rug.

DYEING FOR RUG MAKING

❖

SHIRLEY SIMPSON

Most professional rug hookers dye at least some of the fabrics they use. In this way
they can obtain the colors they need for a particular project. Also, the dyeing
process itself offers its own creative satisfactions—and occasional surprises. The
variation in tone that can be produced (or may happen accidentally) enhances the
texture of the work, giving it added richness. And fabrics of unpromising hue or
obtrusive pattern can be transformed into useful, even beautiful materials.

There are two basic kinds of dye, natural and synthetic, both available to the home dyer. Many people will instinctively opt for natural dyeing, feeling that it is more in sympathy with current ecological attitudes. The process has an aesthetic as well as a practical appeal: materials are gently simmered to release subtle colors into the fabrics. However, very few of the more interestingly colored dyes are substantive—that is, they must first be mordanted (treated with a solution of a metallic salt, such as alum) in order to yield good, relatively permanent colors.

The natural dye recipes given below make use of materials that are usually available in most homes and do not necessarily require mordanting—dry brown onion skins and tea or coffee bags. They will serve as a "taster" for new dyers. Most libraries will have a selection of books on natural dyeing for those who wish to experiment further. There is a new and very welcome trend which is to abandon the more toxic mordants and to reduce quite dramatically the amount of a "safe" mordant, such as alum, formerly considered desirable for fast dyeing.

Synthetic and chemical dyes pervade our whole visual world. Glance around a room, open the door of your closet, look out into the street at the passing cars. Almost everything will be colored with some form of synthetic dyestuff.

The great period of discovery for dyestuffs for the textile industry was in the second half of the nineteenth century. This has continued up to the present day; as new fibers and fabrics make their appearance, the old formulas have to be adapted or redesigned.

The synthetic dyestuffs recommended for use with the recipes in this chapter have been developed to meet specific commercial requirements within the textile industry, where standards of performance are rigorously monitored.

Acid dyes (specifically acid-leveling dyestuffs) have good light and washfast ratings. They are easy to use in a hot acidulated dyebath and are available commercially in a huge range of colors. A suggestion to help the new dyer is that you restrict yourself to the dyes listed under "Equipment" (see page 26). Become very familiar with this palette. Once you have learned to mix dyes together to obtain various colors in white fabric, you can go on to experiment with overdyeing (dyeing on top of an already dyed fabric); the wonderful range of colors that will appear will help to individualize your rag rugs, making them uniquely yours.

You can also try the very much newer fiber-reactive dyes for wool—said to represent a considerable step forward in dyestuff permanence on wool and wool blends. These, too, are used in a hot acid dyebath. The color range is more limited than for acid dyes, but the colors are wonderfully clear. Both of these dyestuffs are normally available from craft shops specializing in requirements for weavers, spinners, and textile artists. They are usually packaged in ¼ ounce or 1 ounce sizes.

Store them in a dry, dark environment until you are ready to use them.

❖ EQUIPMENT ❖

Much of the equipment required for dyeing can be found in your kitchen. However, you will need to buy spares of most items in order to have separate implements for dyeing only (see "Safety for home dyers"). Happily most of them are inexpensive. If you later take up dyeing on a large scale, you may find that you need more specialized equipment, but the following items will be quite adequate at the outset.

◆ **For stirring and manipulating** hot, wet fabrics and yarns, chopsticks—wooden or plastic—are ideal, as are wooden spoons. Because wood will stain, and dye from one spoon might bleed into another color, you should aim to built up a collection to accommodate the most familiar dye colors: red, blue, yellow, and black, as well as other often-used shades such as turquoise and magenta. Spoons and chopsticks can also be used for mixing dyestocks.

◆ **For measuring and weighing** dye powders, dyestocks, and fabrics you will need several different implements: one or more spoons, measuring beakers, and scales.

An ordinary metal teaspoon can be used for measuring dye powders and dyestock solutions, but make sure always to use the same spoon; they do vary slightly. And keep it separate from those used for eating. Alternatively, use a set of measuring spoons, the kind used in cooking: ¼ teaspoon, ½ teaspoon, 1 teaspoon, and 1 tablespoon.

Graduated plastic measuring beakers—3½ ounce and 1¾ ounce—are very useful for quick measuring of small amounts of dyestocks.

A 2 pint graduated measuring beaker is essential. This should be boilproof and ideally should have the measurements clearly visible on the outside.

Kitchen scales are useful for weighing fabrics to be dyed. Bathroom scales can be used, although they are less suitable for weighing small amounts.

SAFETY FOR HOME DYERS

All types of dyeing involve the use of chemical substances. These must not be allowed to come into contact with foodstuffs or areas where food is handled. The following safety precautions should be observed:

◆ **Ventilate the kitchen or working area.**

◆ **Remember not to smoke, drink, or eat while you are dyeing!**

◆ **Completely clear the working area.** This includes removing coffee mugs, sugar bowls, salt shakers, teapots, milk pitchers—*everything*. Cover the work surface completely with newspaper and confine your dyeing to this one prepared area. When you have finished, fold the newspaper and dispose of it. Wash the work surfaces and the top of the stove. Wash your hands.

◆ **Dyeing equipment needs to be identified.** Mark it with nail polish or a waterproof pen, and store it all together, making a mental note that this equipment *must not* be used for anything other than dyeing. If you have children, a written note is advisable. If they are toddlers, store it out of reach.

◆ **Exercise great care with simmering dyebaths.** They are a potential hazard especially for children and elderly people.

◆ **It makes good sense to wear an old shirt or apron when dyeing.** Also wear fine plastic or rubber gloves to protect your hands. When handling any dye powders wear a dust mask (obtainable inexpensively from D.I.Y. stores).

◆ **A dyebath** can initially be improvised from a large old saucepan; it should have a top diameter of 8–10 inches. If you become addicted to dyeing (which often happens!) you may find it worthwhile to invest in the largest stainless steel or enameled dyebath that you can afford. Catering equipment suppliers are a good source of large pans and cauldrons.

A roasting/baking pan, or something of similar size, measuring approximately 16 x 12 x 2–3 inches, is ideal for spot dyeing larger pieces of fabric, either on a burner or in the stove.

◆ **A thermometer** is a great help in achieving successful dyeing. Both time and fuel can be saved by checking the temperature of a dyebath. Thermometers (calibrated to 220°F) can be bought from some cooking equipment stores. Or you can use a thermometer of the kind used for jam making and deep fat frying (restricting it henceforward for dyeing).

◆ **The heat source** may be the gas or electric stove in your kitchen, or you may prefer to use an outside utility/wash house area for your dyeing, perhaps equipped with a hot plate or a portable gas stove, the type used in camping.

This corner of the dyeing workroom contains assorted dyestuffs and, in the foreground, bottles of dyestock solutions.

◆ **For storing the dyestock solutions** glass and/or plastic bottles are needed; plastic has the advantage of being lighter weight and unbreakable. A funnel is useful for pouring the solution into bottles. You will also need stick-on labels for identifying each solution.

❖ DYESTOCK SOLUTIONS ❖

The acid and fiber-reactive dyestuffs mentioned earlier are usually supplied in powder or very fine granular form. They will mix easily with water to form a dyestock solution. This can be stored for convenience in a clean glass or plastic bottle, preferably in a cool, dark closet or cabinet. Such solutions are always at hand ready for immediate use. They will remain viable for at least one year.

In addition to the dye itself and the water, you will need some vinegar. This is added to the water in a dyebath to help fix the color and thus is termed an "acid dyeing assistant"; it contains 4–5 percent acetic acid. White vinegar is usually recommended for dyeing because it is colorless, but ordinary cider vinegar is adequate for dark materials.

Estimating the amount to use is a simple process. Take the weight of the fabric you are using and halve that number. For example, if your fabric weighs 4 ounces, allow 2 ounces (approximately 3 tablespoons) of vinegar.

To prepare 2 pints of stock solution:

1. Put 2 teaspoons of dyestuff in a measuring jug. Add 1 or 2 drops of dishwashing detergent.

2. Mix the powder to a smooth paste using a little boiling water.

3. Slowly add hot water to make 2 pints exactly. Stir well with a wooden spoon.

4. Let the dye cool, then bottle and label it (e.g. "RED: Sept. 25, 1995").

This quantity of dyestock solution will dye a total weight of 2.2 pounds of fabric or yarn to a medium shade of the color.

❖ COLOR MIXING ❖

Once stock solutions are mixed in readiness for dyeing, try experimenting with them as paints to learn how to put colors together. Collect together half a dozen small empty jars or yogurt tubs, an old white plate, an inexpensive paintbrush, a few sheets of white paper, and an eyedropper.

Pour a small amount of one dyestock into an empty jar. Fill another jar with rinsing water. Using the paintbrush dipped into the dyestock—perhaps yellow—paint a small square on the paper. Rinse the brush and repeat with blue. Now make green by mixing a drop of yellow and a drop of blue dyestock together. Paint this color next to the painted samples of yellow and blue and label it "Yellow 1, Blue 1."

This very simple technique will enable you to see for yourself exactly what happens when you mix colors together. By varying the proportions, you will alter both the color and the intensity of the dye mix. Use these painted experiments as an indication of the type of color you will achieve, rather than an exact reproduction. Remember also that your testings are likely to have been carried out on white paper. If you dye recycled fabrics, the base color will affect the finished result.

Build up a collection of these labeled painted squares. They will be very helpful when you start dyeing for a particular project.

Similarly, when you begin dyeing fabrics, keep a record of the undyed and dyed fabrics. Just a small square of fabric stapled into a notebook will be very helpful. If you record the weight of the fabric dyed and brief details of the dyestocks used, you will be able to repeat or match up a particularly successful batch of dyeing; this will prove invaluable when you are working on a large project.

❖ PREPARING FABRICS FOR DYEING ❖

New wool or wool-blend fabrics. Either wash the fabric by hand in hot water and detergent or put it through a moderately hot wash cycle in your washing machine.

Recycled wool fabrics. Old woolen blankets will need to be washed, as described above. They can then be torn into pieces. A useful size for dyeing is 10 x 16 inches. Hems, selvages, and worn areas should be cut off before dyeing—they may be less apparent after dyeing and might spoil the appearance of the rug. But don't throw these scraps away; they will be very useful later for test dyeings.

Wool and wool-blend. Clothing, including knitwear, should be cut into usable pieces and washed before dyeing.

❖ THE DYEING PROCESS ❖

The following recipes will enable you to achieve a great range of colors and different effects.

Recipe 1: Overdyeing (for even color) recycled woolens—woven and knitted

1. Collect together approximately 8 ounces woolen fabrics. For these early dyeings it is interesting to dye some colored fabrics as well as a piece of white woolen fabric, perhaps part of an old blanket. The white fabric will indicate the true dye color after dyeing, while the assorted colored pieces will provide some surprises. Before dyeing, identify each piece with a label written in ballpoint pen on masking tape and attached with rust-proof safety pins.

2. Fill a bucket with warm water and add one or two drops of dishwashing detergent. Stir. Add the woolen fabrics, and allow them to soak for one hour prior to dyeing.

3. Prepare the dyebath. Measure out the appropriate quantities of water, vinegar, and dyestock solution.
Water: multiply the weight of the dry fabric, in ounces, by 30. The result, in fluid ounces, is the required amount of water. For example, 30 x 7 ounces = 210 fluid ounces or 13 pints.
Vinegar: divide the weight of the fabric by two; in this example, the required amount of vinegar would be 3½ fluid ounces.
Dyestock solution: for medium colors, equalize the

weight of the fabric with the volume of dyestock; that is, use the same figure of fluid ounces as you have of ounces. Thus, for 7 ounces of fabric, allow 7 fluid ounces of solution. This can consist either of one color or of a mixture of two or three dyes totalling 7 fluid ounces.

Put the water, vinegar, and dyestock(s) into the dyebath. Stir thoroughly.

4. Squeeze the water from the soaking fabrics. Open them out and add them to the dyebath. Push the fabric into the dye solution as quickly as possible. Heat the dyebath *slowly* to a gentle simmer (at approximately 176°F), allowing 30–45 minutes for this. Stir *gently* every 5–10 minutes.

5. Hold the dyebath at this temperature for another 45–60 minutes, stirring occasionally.

6. Turn off the heat and allow dyebath and contents to cool completely.

7. Rinse the fabric in tepid water and repeat until the water is clear. Spin the fabric in the washing machine or a spin dryer or roll it in towels.

There will not be any usable dye remaining in the bath. Dilute the residue with plenty of cold water and dispose of it down an outside drain.

Recipe 1 can be summarized as follows:

Water required: 30 x fabric weight

Vinegar: half fabric weight

Dye solutions:
- ◆ *medium color:* equalize weight of the fabric with volume of dyestocks.
- ◆ *dark colors:* equalize weight of the fabric with twice volume of dyestocks.
- ◆ *pale colors:* equalize weight of the fabric with half volume of dyestocks.

The recipe can doubled or tripled for greater weights of fabric.

This piece of striped fabric has been overdyed with blue to produce two shades of blue.

The variegated blue background of this rug was achieved by using overdyed fabric similar to that shown above.

If you follow these instructions carefully, you should obtain an evenly colored piece of fabric. If the effect is mottled, it may be because you have
- ◆ failed to get the fabric thoroughly wet before immersing it in the dyebath
- ◆ not used enough dye solution
- ◆ hurried the heating process; the dyebath must be heated very slowly and held simmering for at least 45 minutes.

Recipe 2: Random dyeing

This method produces wonderfully variegated effects, which are excellent for obtaining several shades of one color—useful especially in backgrounds. For it you will need a rectangular baking pan.

1. Weigh the fabric (try to start with a conveniently round figure, say 4 ounces). Soak it for at least one hour in a bucket of warm water containing one or two drops of dishwashing detergent.

2. Put 2 pints of warm water in the baking pan. Add 1¾ fluid ounces (about three tablespoons) vinegar (half the figure for the fabric weight).

3. Measure out the dyestock(s).
◆ *For a single-colored random effect,* measure 5¼ fluid ounces of dyestock into a measuring jug.
◆ *For a multicolored random effect,* select three different colors (such as red, blue, and yellow), and put varying amounts of dyestock into three empty jars or yogurt tubs. For example, try 3½ fluid ounces red, 1¾ fluid ounces blue, ⅔ fluid ounces yellow.

4. Squeeze the surplus water from the soaking fabric and place it in the baking pan, crumpling it to fit.

5. Slowly pour the measured dyestock over the fabric. Allow the dyestock to find its own level, but a little pushing around with a chopstick may be necessary. If you are using two or more colors, they will mix together to make beautiful patterns.
Do not attempt to even out the dye on the fabric. To some extent this will happen naturally.

6. Cover the dyebath with aluminum foil. Pierce the foil once or twice with a chopstick.

7. Heat the dyebath *very slowly* on the burner to simmering point at approximately 176°F over a period of 20–30 minutes.

8. Allow the bath to simmer at this temperature for another 15–20 minutes. Turn off the heat.

9. Allow the fabric to cool completely in the dyebath. All or most of the dyestock will have been taken up by the fabric. Rinse the fabric in tepid water.

Recipe 3: Natural dyeing using onion skins

Natural dyeing is somewhat less predictable and reliable than chemical dyeing. Even such commodities as onion skins and tea leaves will yield variable amounts of dye coloring; but it is this very unpredictability that makes natural dyeing so enjoyable.

1. For approximately 4 ounces of fabric you will need a generous 1 ounce of dry brown onion skins and 1¾ fluid ounces vinegar.

2. Put the fabric to soak in a bucket of warm water containing one or two drops of dishwashing detergent. Soak for at least one hour.

3. Put the onion skins in the dyebath. Cover them with 2 pints of water. Bring the mixture slowly to simmering point. Simmer for 30–45 minutes. Cool. Strain off the dye liquor, which should be bright yellow, and reserve it. Rinse the dyebath.

4. Put approximately 5½ pints of water into the rinsed dyebath. Add 1¾ fluid ounces vinegar and the dye liquor, then stir thoroughly.

5. Remove the soaking fabric from the bucket. Squeeze out the surplus water. Open out the fabric and add it to the dyebath. Bring the dyebath to simmering point (176°F) over 20–30 minutes. Hold it there for another 30–40 minutes, stirring occasionally.

6. Either allow the fabric to cool in the dyebath or remove it from the dyebath and rinse it when cool.

The result, on white fabric, will be a bright, clear orange-yellow. Experiment with different fabrics. Note that blue fabrics, for example, can be "greened" by putting them in this dyebath.

Recipe 4: Natural dyeing with tea or coffee bags

Prepare the fabric and dyebath as described for recipe 3. Experiment with different numbers of tea/coffee bags (start with five), preparing the dye liquor as for the onion skins. Unless large numbers of bags are used, the liquor will tint rather than dye the fabric, producing various tones of fawn or beige.

This recipe can also be used to tone down bright fabrics or the result of overbright synthetic dyeing.
Note: These natural dyes will not be as colorfast as synthetic dyes.

THE PROJECTS

Swiss Check

❖

OLGA ROTHSCHILD

An underlying pattern of squares provides an appropriately tidy structure for
this impression of a typical Swiss landscape, with its chalet,
outbuildings, forests, and fields. The rushing, twisting river gives the illusion
that one is looking at a mountainside—as well as providing a
strongly unifying element. The relative importance of the chalet is shown by
its position and by the fact that it occupies two squares of the grid.
Some of the fields, too, spill over into an adjacent square,
helping to prevent the design from being static.

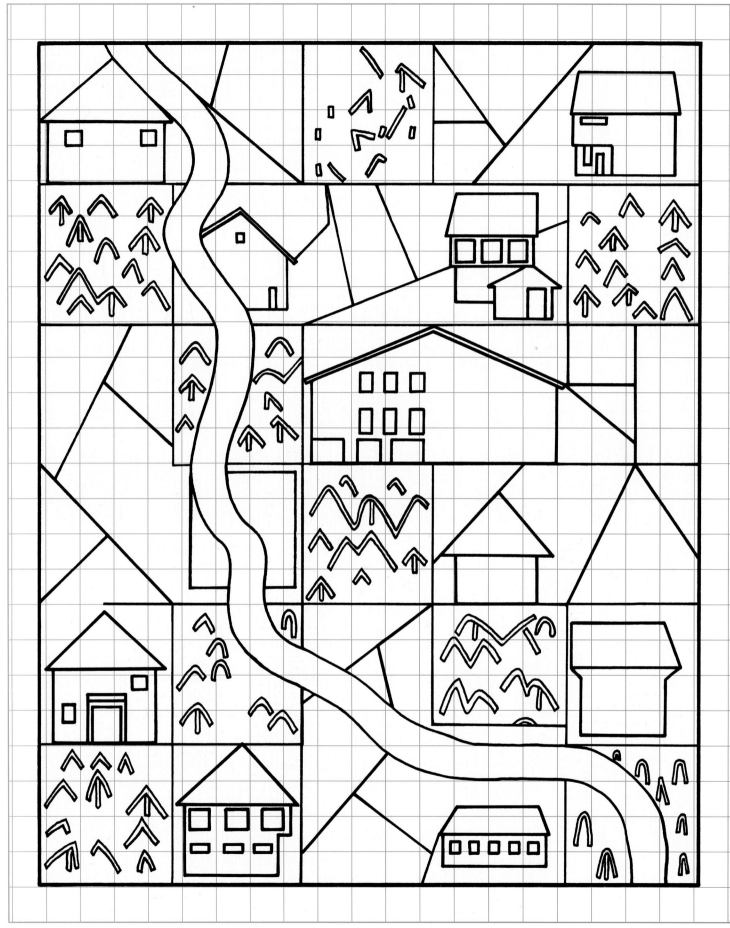

One square = 2 inches

The many shades of green in this rug give it a special richness. Five shades are listed in Materials, below, but you can achieve more variety if you dye the fabrics yourself and exploit the accidental variation that this produces. Otherwise, an old green tweed jacket would be perfect.

SIZE
47 x 39 inches

MATERIALS
Wool fabrics in the following colors and approximate quantities
(based on 60 inch fabric):

- forest green . . . . 1⅜ yards
- chartreuse . . . . ⅝ yard
- bottle green . . . . ⅜ yard
- olive green . . . . ⅜ yard
- pale chartreuse . . . . ¼ yard
- dark gray . . . . ¾ yard
- pale green-gray . . . . ⅝ yard
- dark brown . . . . ½ yard
- white . . . . ¼ yard
- medium brown tweed . . ⅛ yard
- black . . . . ⅛ yard
- red . . . . ⅛ yard

Piece of burlap or coarse linen 53 x 45 inches

5⅛ yards of rug-binding tape

Linen or carpet thread and large needle

Hand hook

Frame

❖

INSTRUCTIONS

1. Zigzag-stitch or overcast the edges of the backing fabric.

2. Transfer the design to the fabric using your chosen method (see pages 17–19).

3. Mount the fabric in the frame (see page 19).

4. Cut strips of fabric ¼ inch wide.

5. Work the hooking as described on pages 20–21, following the photograph as a guide to color placement. The fields and buildings are worked mainly in horizontal rows—some in vertical rows. The hooking of the river should naturally follow the flow. For the border, work one or two rows of black, then fill in the outer edges with brown, gray, and touches of red.

6. Check the rug to make sure that there are no gaps, then block it as described on page 22.

7. Bind the edges with tape as described on pages 22–23.

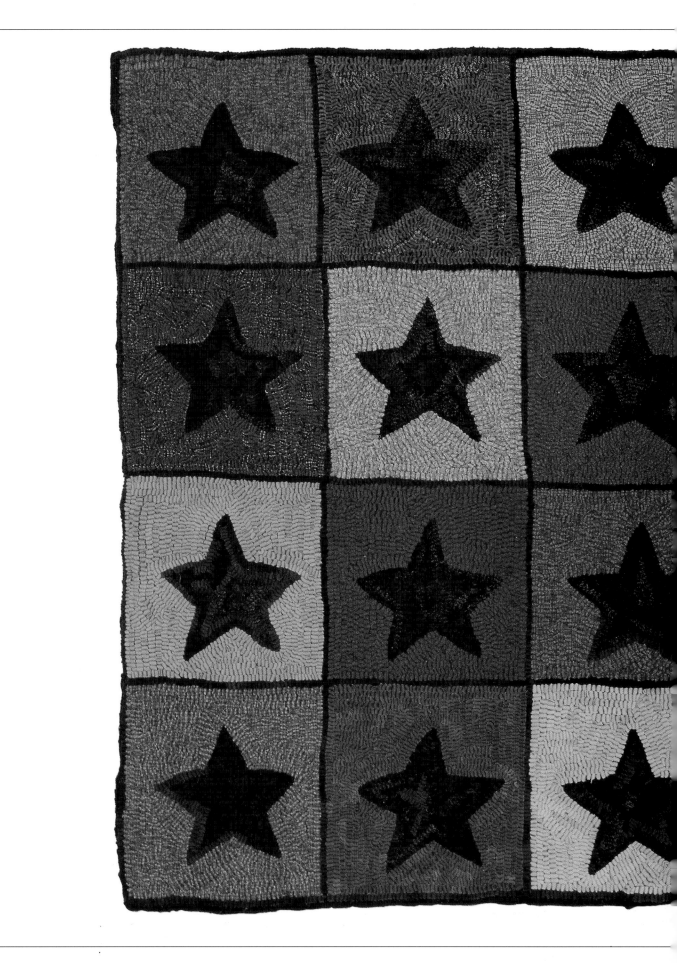

STARS

❖

POLLY MINICK

Simplicity and subtlety are the keynotes of this appealing rug. All of the fabrics (recycled wools) were hand dyed to produce a beautifully harmonious palette of muted shades—apart from the cherry red, which gives the design a "lift." Polly Minick devotes a lot of time to getting the colors just right. She saves dyeing for the summer, when it's too hot to do the hooking (she works on a hoop held in her lap). A cauldron filled with some of her "witch's brew" can then be found bubbling away in the garden.

This design could be adapted to any size you like: add more squares for a larger rug or make just four for a pillow cover. Notice that the black stars are not solid black but several tones of black and dark gray. A full-size trace pattern is provided for a single star. When you are transferring it to the fabric, trace the star fairly roughly to produce the spontaneous look the designer has achieved.

Star template

SIZE
36 x 45 inches

MATERIALS
Wool fabrics in the following colors and approximate quantities
(based on 60 inch fabric):

◆ shades of black
  and gray . . . . .1½ yards
◆ cinnamon . . . . .⅜ yard
◆ purple-gray . . . . .⅜ yard
◆ beige . . . . .⅜ yard
◆ golden beige . . . . .⅜ yard
◆ gray-blue . . . . .⅜ yard
◆ grape . . . . .⅜ yard
◆ medium brown . . . . .¼ yard
◆ wheat . . . . .¼ yard
◆ brick red . . . . .¼ yard
◆ dark brick red . . . . .¼ yard
◆ cherry red . . . . .¼ yard
◆ cream . . . . .¼ yard
◆ light brown . . . . .¼ yard
◆ gray-brown . . . . .¼ yard

Piece of burlap 42 x 51 inches

4⅞ yards of rug-binding tape

Linen or carpet thread and large needle

Hand hook

Frame

❖

INSTRUCTIONS

1. Zigzag-stitch or overcast the edges of the backing fabric.

2. Mark the design area (finished size of rug) on the burlap and divide it into twenty 9-inch squares. Trace the full-size star provided; glue it to cardboard and cut it out. Use this template to draw the stars in each square.

3. Mount the fabric in the frame (see page 19).

4. Cut strips of fabric ⅜ inch wide.

5. Work the hooking as described on pages 20–21, following the photograph as a guide to color placement—or place the colors as you please. Note that the rows immediately adjacent to the black grid lines are straight lines, while those around the star follow its shape. Fill the intervening spaces as you like.

6. Check the rug to make sure that there are no gaps, then block it as described on page 22.

7. Bind the edges with tape as described on pages 22–23.

Tumbling Cats

❖

Joan Dennis
Based on a design by Dahlov Ipcar

A cat in front of the fire—in one form or another, from contented purring puss to
defunct tiger's skin—has long symbolized "home." This splendid tiger and leopard,
depicted in loving detail against lush jungle foliage, take the idea in a new
direction. The design, adapted from a rug by an American woman artist, Dahlov
Ipcar, evokes the work of Henri ("Le Douanier") Rousseau. Most of the fabrics were
hand dyed. Astonishingly, this was Joan Dennis's first attempt at dyeing;
she found that it was "almost as much fun as the hooking."

To get the subtle variation of tones for the cats and the greens for the foliage, Joan Dennis overdyed several rust, gold, and green wool fabrics, using both commercial dyes and red and yellow onion skins. She used a technique known as casserole dyeing, stuffing the dyepot with fabrics and dye and then baking it in the oven. (The quantities given below are for usable strips; you may need more fabric in order to select the tones you wish to use.) For the leaf veins she used a finely patterned dark brown plaid; a bolder plaid, using shades of red, green, and purple on a brown background, was used for the background.

SIZE
34 x 51½ inches

MATERIALS
Wool fabrics in the following colours and approximate quantities
(based on 60 inch fabric):

- shades of gold . . . . . . .1⅛ yards
- shades of rust . . . . .¾ yard
- shades of brown . . . . . . .½ yard
- shades of green . . . . . .1⅛ yards
- dark brown plaid . . . . . .⅞ yard
- small-patterned
  brown plaid . . . . .¼ yard
- black . . . . .¼ yard

Piece of burlap 40 x 58 inches

5 yards of rug-binding tape

Linen or carpet thread and large needle

Hand hook

Frame

❖

INSTRUCTIONS

1. Zigzag-stitch or oversew the edges of the backing fabric.

2. Transfer the design to the fabric using your chosen method (see pages 17–19).

3. Mount the fabric in the frame (see page 19).

4. Cut strips of fabric ¼ inch wide.

5. Work the hooking as described on pages 20–21, following the photographs as guides to color placement and patterns of hooking. Work the border in the darkest shade of green.

6. Check the rug to make sure that there are no gaps, then block it as described on page 22.

7. Bind the edges with the tape as described on pages 22–23.

One square = 2 inches

FRAKTUR WATERCOLOR

— ❖ —

BETH SNYDER

Old Pennsylvania German documents called Frakturs were decorated with watercolors of stylized birds and flowers. A Fraktur bookplate served as the inspiration for this charming design. The subtle shading achieved in the birds' bodies and wings, the blue parts of the flower, and the leaves was achieved by using a manufacturer's woolen swatches, which come in packs of six shades of the same color. For a similar effect, try using a single shade of dye and leaving the fabric in the dyebath for different lengths of time. If dyeing your own colors, aim for five shades of gold and four each of blue and green.

SIZE
34 x 25 inches

MATERIALS
Wool fabric in the following colors and approximate quantities
(based on 60 inch fabric):

- pale gray . . . . .2 yards
- dark gold . . . . ½ yard
- gold . . . . ½ yard
- yellow . . . . ½ yard
- rose . . . . ½ yard
- tan . . . . ¼ yard
- white . . . . ¼ yard
- shaded gold . . . . ⅜ yard
- shaded azure blue . . . . . .⅜ yard
- shaded dark green . . . . . ⅜ yard

Piece of burlap 40 x 31 inches

3½ yards of rug-binding tape

Linen or carpet thread and large needle

Hand hook   Frame

— ❖ —

INSTRUCTIONS

1. Zigzag-stitch or overcast the edges of the backing fabric.
2. Transfer the design to the fabric (see pages 17–19).
3. Cut strips of fabric ¼ inch wide.
4. Work the hooking as described on pages 20–21, following the photograph as a guide to color placement. Graduate the shades of gold on the birds' bodies, and follow the shading for the blue and green on the wings, heads, flowers, and leaves.
5. Check the rug to make sure that there are no gaps, then block it as described on page 22.
6. Bind the edges as described on pages 22–23.

One square = 2 inches

MC²

❖

OLGA ROTHSCHILD

The familiar woven-check tablecloth found in bistros everywhere
provided the inspiration for this sophisticated rug in black, white,
and shades of gray tweed, enlivened by touches of scarlet.

To achieve the effect of a gingham tablecloth, where the dark and light threads cross to produce a tint, Olga Rothschild used gray tweed, recycled from two mens' jackets—one a dark gray and one a lighter gray. The white is actually a very pale gray-green, which harmonizes better with the tweeds than a pure white would. She used a pure red for the borders and a red plaid for the spots, which gives a subtler effect. If you wish to create a similar effect, divide the amount given below for red by two: one lot for each red.

SIZE
29½ x 28 inches

MATERIALS
Wool fabrics in the following colors and approximate quantities
(based on 60 inch fabric):

◆ black and white tweed . . . . .⅝ yard

◆ white and black tweed . . . . .⅝ yard

◆ black . . . . .¾ yard

◆ white . . . . .½ yard

◆ red . . . . .⅛ yard

Piece of burlap 36 x 34 inches

3½ yards of rug-binding tape

Linen or carpet thread and large needle

Hand hook

Frame

❖

INSTRUCTIONS

1. Zigzag-stitch or overcast the edges of the backing fabric.
2. Mark a square 28 x 28 inches on the backing fabric, and then divide it into forty-nine 4-inch squares. Mark a small square in the center of every alternate square, as shown. Add ¾ inch to the top and bottom edges.
3. Mount the fabric in a frame (see page 19).
4. Cut strips of fabric ¼ in wide.
5. Work the hooking as described on pages 20–21, working in straight lines. For the borders, work one row of red, one of black.
6. Check the rug to make sure that there are no gaps, then block it as described on page 22.
7. Bind the edges with tape as described on pages 22–23.

THREE MARANS

❖

EMMA TENNANT

This handsome breed of chicken is popular, says Emma Tennant, because they lay enormous eggs, although they are not as productive as modern breeds. The roosters (a lighter shade of gray than the hens) "rule their roosts with fierce authority," she says. This one occupies center stage against a background of gently sloping Scottish Lowland hills and a serene blue sky.

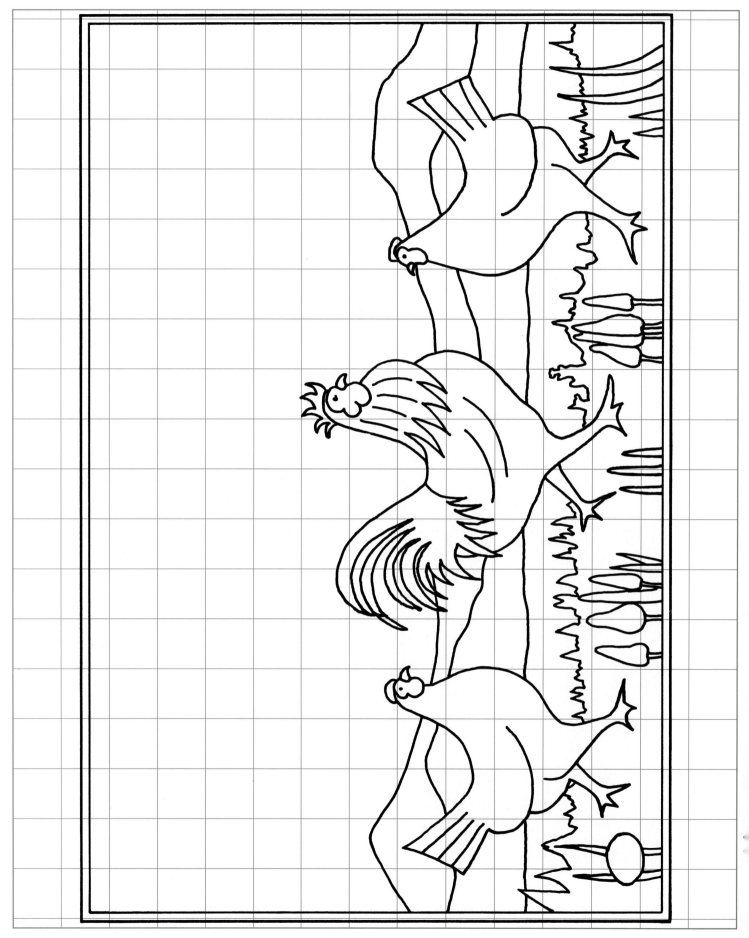

For the feathers of these birds, tweed fabrics are ideal, says the designer; herringbone is particularly good. The harmonious shades of the sky can be achieved by dyeing with the same shade at different strengths.

SIZE
24 x 36 inches

MATERIALS
Wool fabrics in the following colors and approximate quantities
(based on 60 inch fabric):

- 3 shades of azure blue . . . . .1⅛ yards
- dark gray tweed . . . . . . .⅜ yard
- medium gray tweed . . . . .¼ yard
- light gray tweed . . . . . . .⅛ yard
- emerald green . . . . .¼ yard
- light green . . . . .⅛ yard
- dark green . . . . .⅛ yard
- blue-green . . . . .⅛ yard
- forest green . . . . .⅛ yard
- red . . . . .⅛ yard
- 2 shades of mauve . . . . . .scraps
- pale yellow . . . . .scrap
- white . . . . .scrap
- charcoal gray . . . . .scrap

Piece of burlap 30 x 42 inches

3½ yards of rug-binding tape

Linen or carpet thread and large needle

Hand hook

Frame

--- ❖ ---

INSTRUCTIONS

1. Zigzag-stitch or overcast the edges of the backing fabric.
2. Transfer the design to the fabric using your chosen method (see pages 17–19).
3. Mount the fabric in the frame (see page 19).
4. Cut strips of fabric ½ inch wide.
5. Work the hooking as described on pages 20–21, following the photograph as a guide to color placement. Note that the sky is hooked in horizontal rows, the foreground in vertical rows. In hooking the hills and the birds, follow the natural contours.
6. Check the rug to make sure that there are no gaps, then block it as described on page 22.
7. Bind the edges with the tape as described on pages 22–23.

BIRD ON THE VINE

❖

HAPPY AND STEVE DiFRANZA

This perky little bird of indeterminate species is surrounded by a
feast of grapes and strawberries. The undulating lines of the vine
recall the borders found in eighteenth- and early nineteenth-century
embroidered samplers. Usually worked in cross stitch, these tend
to have a slightly angular quality, whereas hooking, which can be
worked in any direction, is ideally suited to depicting
curved shapes and lines.

For the two-tone green border of this rug and for the background and vine, the DiFranzas dyed their own fabrics. They used the same green dye for the border, using a stronger solution for one lot, to obtain two different shades. If you prefer, you could use a dark background, instead of cream. Make sure, however, that the other colors are light and vibrant enough to show up well against it.

SIZE
20 x 30 inches

MATERIALS
Wool fabrics in the following colors and approximate quantities
(based on 60 inch fabric):

◆ cream . . . . .¾ yard   ◆ green tweed . . . . .⅛ yard
◆ blue . . . . .⅛ yard   ◆ lavender . . . . .⅛ yard
◆ brown . . . . .⅛ yard   ◆ red . . . . .⅛ yard
◆ light green . . . . .⅛ yard   ◆ gold . . . . . . .piece 3 x 13 inches
◆ dark green . . . . .⅛ yard   ◆ black . . . . . .1 strip ⅛ x 8 inches

Piece of burlap or coarse linen, 26 x 36 inches

3 yards of rug-binding tape

Linen or carpet thread and large needle

Hand hook   Frame

❖

INSTRUCTIONS

1. Zigzag-stitch or overcast the edges of the backing fabric.
2. Transfer the design to the fabric using your chosen method (see pages 17–19)
3. Mount the fabric in the frame (see page 19).
4. Cut strips of fabric ⅛ inch wide.
5. Work the hooking as described on pages 20–21, following the photograph as a guide to color placement. In working the background, follow the curves of the design; work the border in parallel rows. Add tiny details such as the bird's eye and the strawberry seeds after the surrounding area is hooked.
6. Check the rug to make sure that there are no gaps, then block it as described on page 22.
7. Bind the edges with the tape as described on pages 22–23.

One square = 2 inches

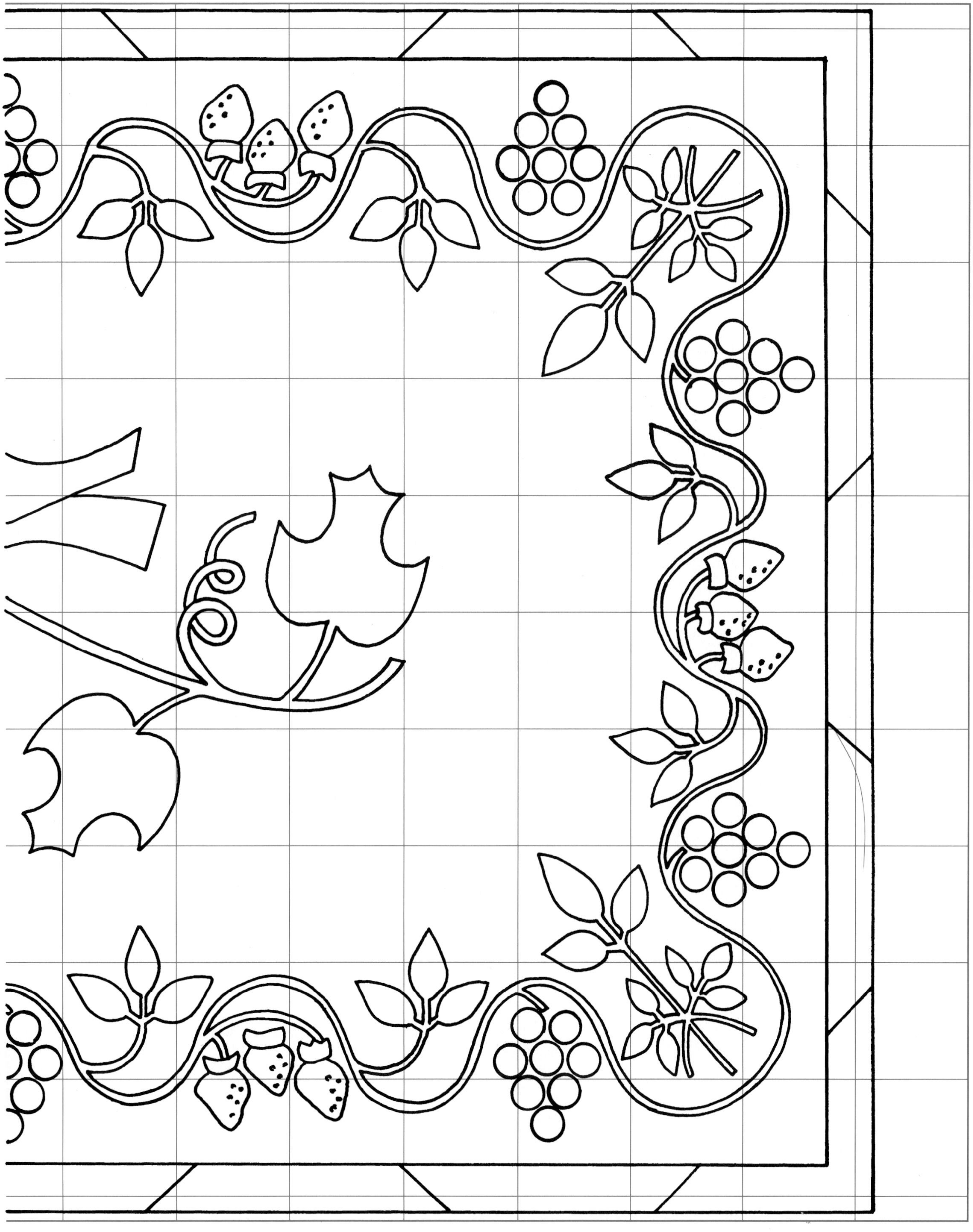

PATCHWORK RUG

❖

HAPPY AND STEVE DiFRANZA

The intriguing shapes of traditional patchwork translate well into hooked rugs. Here, the DiFranzas have taken a simple block and made it dance—by turning it on its "toes" and dressing it in a brilliant range of jewel-like colors. The background enhances the sense of movement, with its subtle shifts from blue to red and back again.

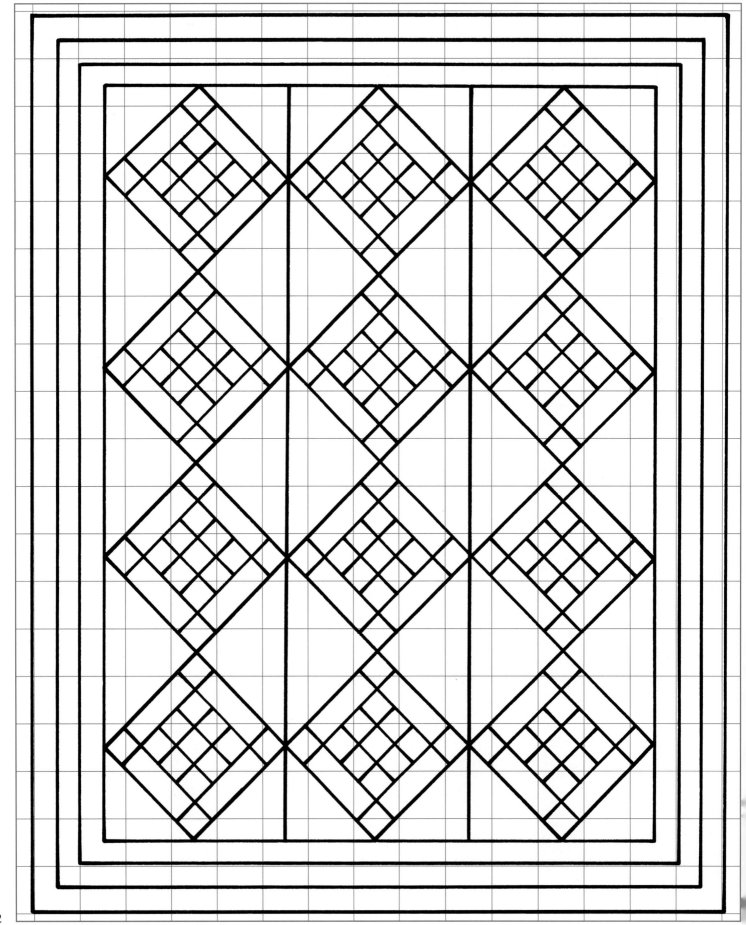

The simple geometric shapes of this rug offer a chance to develop your own feeling for color. Don't try to follow the photograph exactly; in fact, you could choose a completely different palette, if you like. Whichever tones you choose, begin by sorting them into four main groups. This rug uses the following: blues, pinks, rusts/browns and gray/black. You might find it useful to plan your color arrangement on the chart, using colored pencils to match your fabrics, before you begin the hooking.

SIZE
30 x 38 inches

MATERIALS
Wool fabric in the following colors and approximate quantities
(based on 60 inch fabric):

- black . . . . ⅝ yard
- bright rust. . . . . ⅝ yard
- medium blue . . . . ½ yard
- light blue . . . . ¼ yard
- sapphire . . . . ¼ yard
- plum . . . . ¼ yard
- pink. . . . . ⅛ yard
- rust brown . . . . ¼ yard
- light rust . . . . ⅛ yard
- tan. . . . . ¼ yard
- dark gray. . . . . ¼ yard
- light gray. . . . . ⅛ yard
- green . . . . ⅛ yard

Piece of burlap or coarse linen, 36 x 44 inches

4 yards of rug-binding tape

Carpet thread and large needle

Hand hook   Frame

❖

INSTRUCTIONS

1. Zigzag-stitch or overcast the edges of the backing fabric.
2. Transfer the design to the fabric (see pages 17–19). Or, you may prefer to mark out the pattern without using the grid. Each border is 1 inch wide; the three rows in the central rectangle are 8 inches wide; each diamond has a maximum depth of 8 inches.
3. Mount the fabric in the frame (see page 19).
4. Cut strips of fabric ³⁄₁₆ inch wide.
5. Work the hooking as described on pages 20–21, following the photograph as a guide to color placement.
6. Check the rug to make sure that there are no gaps, then block it as described on page 22.
7. Bind the edges with the tape as described on pages 22–23.

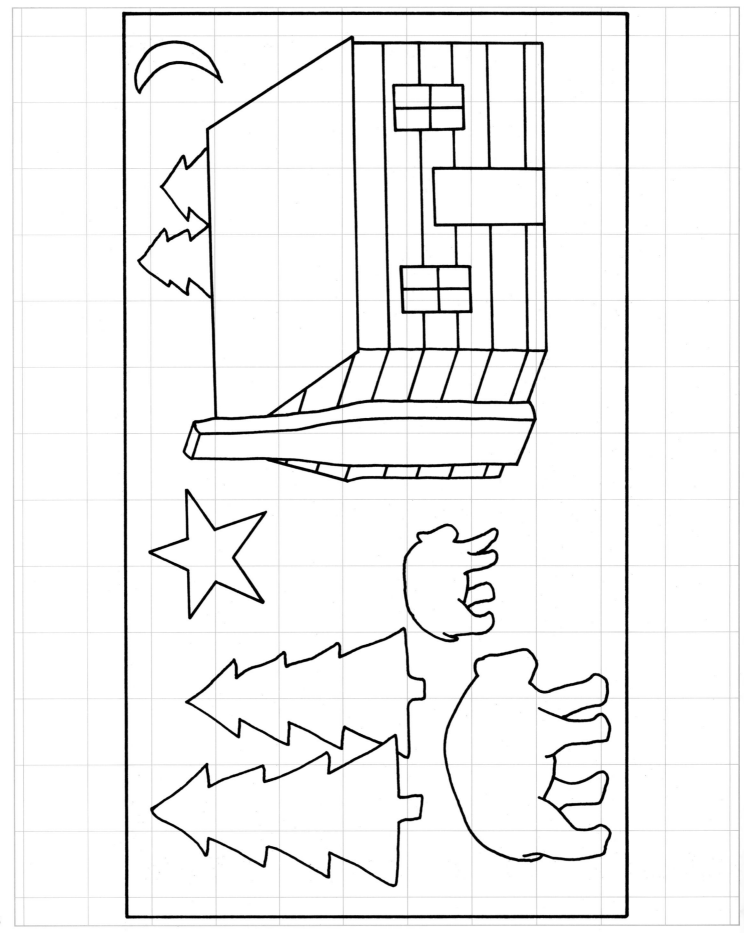

LOG CABIN AND BEARS

— ❖ —

BETH SEKERKA

A haunting quality pervades this simply-rendered scene of a snug log cabin with glowing windows. Like most professional rug designers, Beth uses mainly hand-dyed wool to achieve a rich antique look. She also stresses the importance of using good-quality heavy-duty burlap for the backing.

SIZE
16 x 27 inches

MATERIALS
Wool fabrics in the following colors and approximate quantities
(based on 60 inch fabric):

- pale oatmeal . . . . .⅝ yard
- dark green . . . . .¼ yard
- gray tweed . . . . .¼ yard
- brown . . . . .¼ yard
- brown tweed . . . . .⅛ yard
- gold . . . . .⅛ yard
- off-white . . . . .⅛ yard
- black . . . . .⅛ yard

Piece of burlap 22 x 33 inches

2¾ yards of rug-binding tape

Linen or carpet thread and large needle

Hand hook   Frame

— ❖ —

INSTRUCTIONS

1. Zigzag-stitch or overcast the edges of the backing fabric.
2. Transfer the design to the fabric by chosen method (see pages 17–19).
3. Mount the fabric in the frame (see page 19).
4. Cut strips of fabric ¼ inch wide (slightly thinner for the windows).
5. Work the hooking as described on pages 20–21, following the photograph as a guide to color placement. Note that the house is worked in horizontal and vertical rows, as is the snow where it adjoins the dark green border. Elsewhere the hooking follows the shapes.
6. Check the rug to make sure that there are no gaps, then block it as described on page 22.
7. Bind the edges with the tape as described on pages 22–23.

PARTRIDGE IN A PEAR TREE

❖

ANN DAVIES

Inspired by the many Christmas cards featuring the partridge in its pear tree, Ann Davies created this striking wallhanging, which could also serve as a rug. Most of the fabrics used for this project were hand dyed.

SIZE
31 x 22 inches

MATERIALS
An assortment of wool and other fabrics in the following colors and approximate quantities (based on 60 inch fabric):

- 4 greens from light to dark . . . . .each ¼ yard
- variegated green . . . . . . .¼ yard
- orange-yellow, shaded . . . . .¼ yard
- gray . . . . .⅛ yard
- medium red . . . . .⅛ yard
- purple-green metallic . . . . .⅛ yard
- brown and yellow tweed . . . . .¼ yard
- silver metallic . . . . .scrap

42 ounces of cream knitting worsted (for the background)

Piece of fine burlap 37 x 28 inches

3¼ yards of rug-binding tape, or piece of heavyweight lining fabric 33 x 24 inches and 6 brass rings

Linen or carpet thread and large needle

Hand hook   Frame

❖

INSTRUCTIONS

1. Zigzag-stitch or overcast the edges of the backing fabric.

2. Transfer the design to the fabric (see pages 17–19).

3. Mount the fabric in the frame (see page 19).

4. Cut strips of fabric ³⁄₁₆ inch wide; ⅜ inch wide for the tweed and metallic fabrics.

5. Work the hooking as described on pages 20–21, following the photograph as a guide to color.

6. Check the rug to make sure that there are no gaps, then block it as described on page 22.

7. Bind the edges with the tape as described on pages 22–23. Or, if you are making it as a wallhanging, trim the backing edges to about 1½ inches, turn them under, and glue them in place with fabric glue; sew the lining to the wrong side, then sew the rings to the top edge for hanging from a decorative rod.

One square = 2 inches

BARN RAISING

❖

OLGA ROTHSCHILD

The enduringly popular log cabin patchwork block is reinterpreted here as a
hooked rug. The flexibility of the craft—and the designer's refined color sense—
give the rug an impressionistic character.

Olga Rothschild notes that although the rug looks gray and blue, in fact each square has many colors in it: brown, black, orange, purple, green—and, of course, the traditional red for the "hearth" in the cabin. She began by sorting the wool into piles of light and dark colors. She then made thirty-six piles, one for each square, equally divided between light and dark. After hooking the first square, she made adjustments in color, adding a few lights to the dark and vice versa, to give a warm, rather than sharp, effect in the work. She decided against a border for the rug "because I wanted the mind's eye to carry the design on and on."

SIZE
42 x 42 inches

MATERIALS
A total of 4⅜ yards of wool fabrics
(based on 60 inch fabric),
divided equally into light and dark tones (see above)
and including ⅛ yard of bright red

Piece of burlap or coarse linen 48 inches square

5 yards of carpet-binding tape

Linen or carpet thread and large needle

Hand hook

Frame

❖

INSTRUCTIONS

1. Zigzag-stitch or overcast the edges of the backing fabric.

2. Mark the finished area of the rug on the backing fabric, then divide it into thirty-six 7-inch squares. Draw diagonal lines to divide the squares into light and dark halves. Where the diagonal lines cross, mark a 1 inch square. Around it, mark a few concentric squares to serve as guides for the hooking.

3. Mount the fabric in the frame (see page 19).

4. Cut strips of fabric ¼ inch wide.

5. Work the hooking as described on pages 20–21, using the diagram and photograph as guides for placement of colors.

6. Check the rug to make sure that there are no gaps, then block it as described on page 22.

7. Bind the edges with tape as described on pages 22–23.

SCARECROWS

❖

BARBARA CARROLL
Based on a design by Emma Lou Lais

Neither these three jolly scarecrows nor the cat skulking among the pumpkins seem to hold any terrors for the large red bird perched on one scarecrow's arm, triumphantly brandishing an American flag. Barbara Carroll confesses that she began the rug "with no thought of colors"; the selection evolved as the work progressed. "Each scarecrow became a challenge in using as many different pieces of wool as possible." One inspired choice was a red, white, and blue plaid, which she cut into its separate parts then hooked diagonally to form the strikingly patterned shirt.

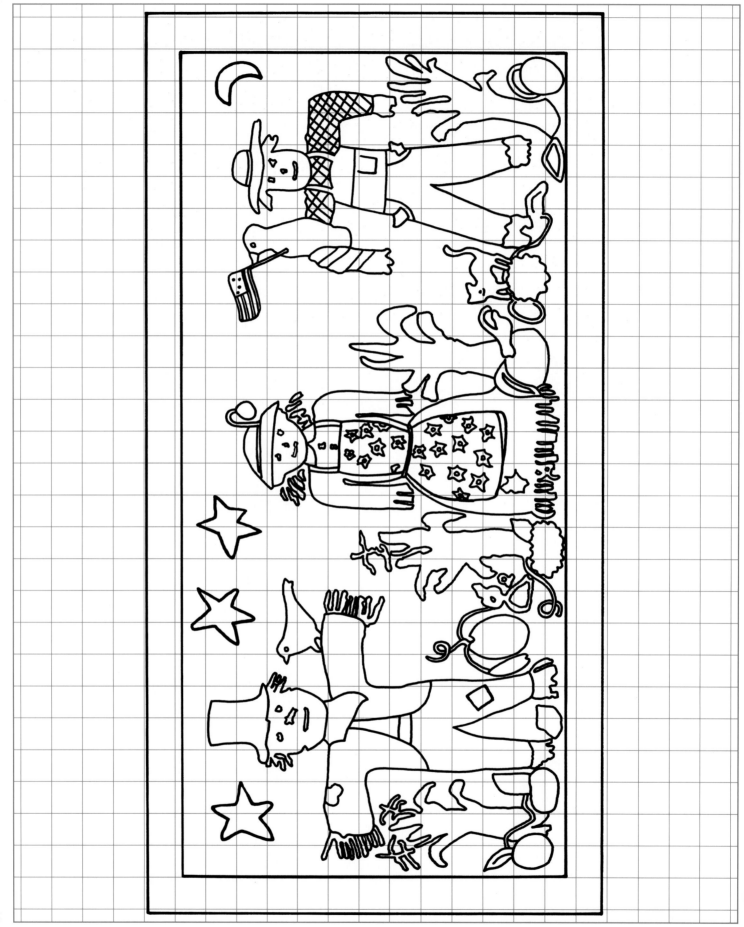

The sky in this rug proves that backgrounds need not be boring. To achieve the rich depth of color, Barbara Carroll used a commercial dye called Antique Brown Black to overdye many shades of gray textured wool fabrics.

SIZE
30½ x 56 inches

MATERIALS
Wool fabrics in the following colors and approximate quantities
(based on 60 inch fabric):

- shades of dark gray . . . 2¼ yards
- shades of blue . . . . ⅞ yard
- shades of brick red . . . . . ½ yard
- blue tweed . . . . ¼ yard
- shades of soft gold . . . . . ¼ yard
- shades of beige . . . . ¼ yard
- cream . . . . ⅛ yard
- red, white, and blue
  plaid . . . . ⅛ yard
- shades of
  gray-green . . . . ⅛ yard
- white . . . . scrap
- light orange . . . . scrap
- bright red . . . . scrap

Piece of monk's cloth or burlap 37 x 62 inches

5⅛ yards of rug-binding tape

Linen or carpet thread and large needle

Hand hook

Frame

❖

INSTRUCTIONS

1. Zigzag-stitch or overcast the edges of the backing fabric.
2. Transfer the design to the fabric using your chosen method (see pages 17–19).
3. Mount the fabric in the frame (see page 19).
4. Cut strips of fabric ¼ inch wide.
5. Work the hooking as described on pages 20–21, following the photographs as guides to color placement. Pay special attention to the sky, hooking in swirling irregular patterns, using the different tones to create the texture.
6. Check the rug to make sure that there are no gaps, then block it as described on page 22.
7. Bind the edges with the tape as described on pages 22–23.

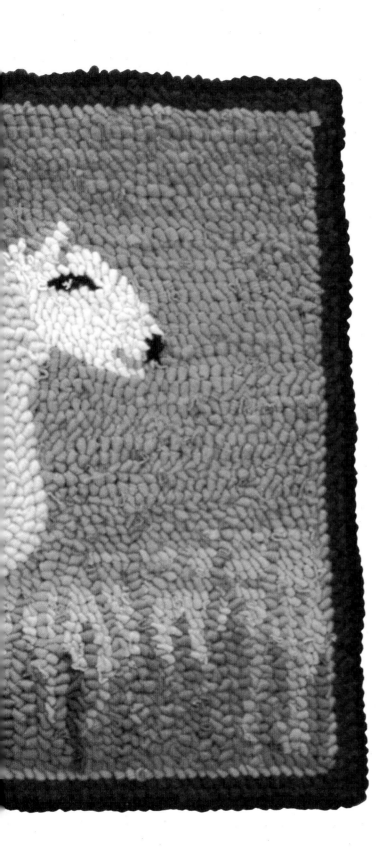

CHEVIOT SHEEP

❖

EMMA TENNANT

Sheep are a perennially popular subject in the decorative arts and lend themselves perfectly to the wool loops of a hooked rug. Emma Tennant's farm boasts a flock of Cheviot sheep, and she has depicted them many times in various surroundings. "This ewe was enjoying the sun on a bright winter's day."

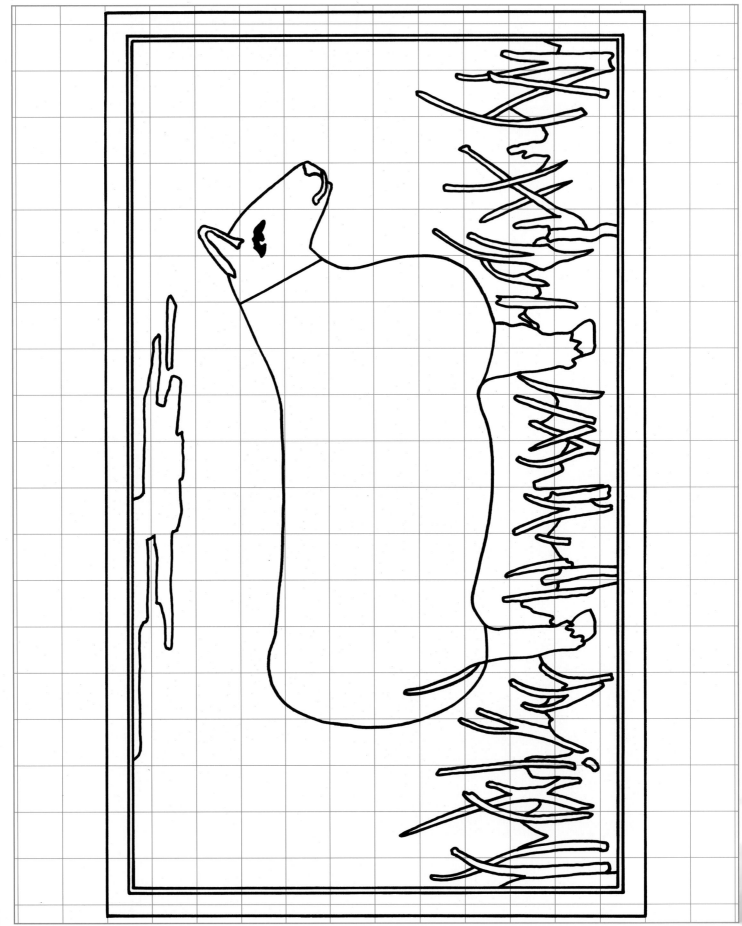

In order to create a thick, fleecy effect, Emma Tennant cut the strips for the sheep's body from an old cream woolen blanket; those for the face and legs she cut from a white sweater. The gold and brown border picks up the colors of the grasses in this wintertime landscape.

SIZE
24 x 38½ inches

MATERIALS
Wool fabrics in the following colors and approximate quantities
(based on 60 inch fabric):

◆ cream . . . . .¾ yard
◆ shades of blue . . . . .1 yard
◆ shades of gold
and beige . . . . .½ yard

◆ dark brown . . . . .¼ yard
◆ white . . . . .¼ yard
◆ gray . . . . .scrap
◆ black . . . . .scrap

Piece of burlap 30 x 44½ inches

3¾ yards of rug-binding tape

Linen or carpet thread and large needle

Hand hook

Frame

❖

INSTRUCTIONS

1. Zigzag-stitch or overcast the edges of the backing fabric.

2. Transfer the design to the fabric using your chosen method (see pages 17–19).

3. Mount the fabric in the frame (see page 19).

4. Cut strips of fabric ½ inch wide.

5. Work the hooking as described on pages 20–21, following the photograph as a guide to color placement. Note the different directions in which the hooking is worked, to suggest, for example, a calm sky, the grasses in the foreground, and the thick wooly coat of the sheep.

6. Check the rug to make sure that there are no gaps, then block it as described on page 22.

7. Bind the edges with the tape as described on pages 22–23.

COTTAGE GARDEN
No. 5

❖

LIZ KITCHING

The designer's own cottage garden, in the Lake District, served as the inspiration for this colorful rug, worked in a marvelous assortment of wool tweeds, suggesting the profusion of plants characteristic of such country gardens. A little discipline is imposed by the diagonal grid background, representing a trellis. The flowers, typifying the unaffected charm of cottage gardens, are set against a patch of clear blue which sets up a sharp contrast with the background.

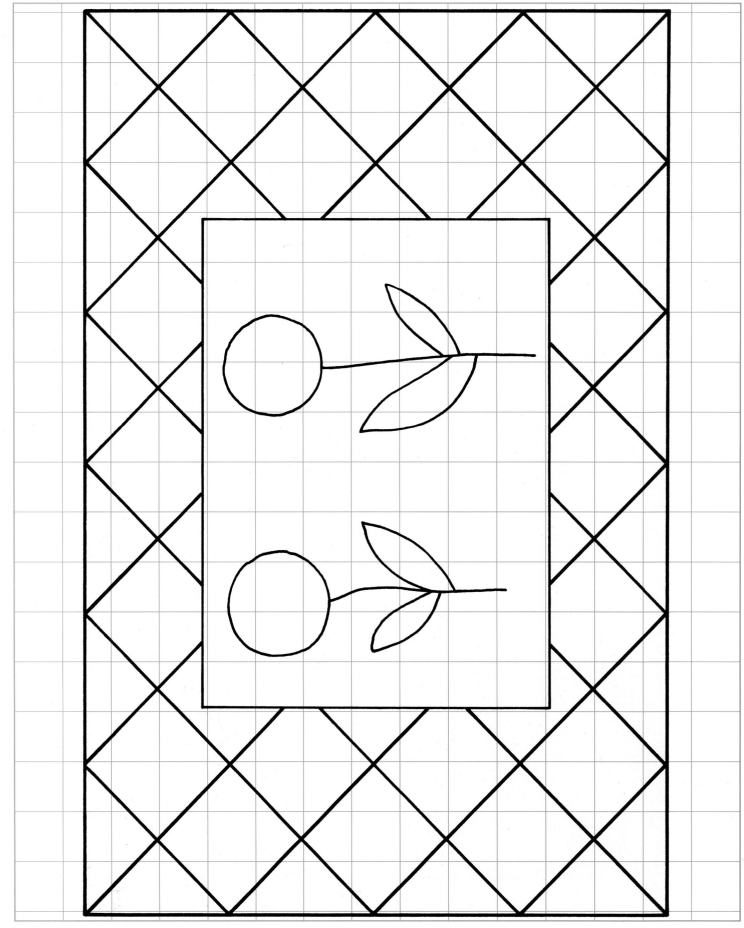

The designer of this rug is fortunate in having access to a local woolen mill, from which she obtains remnants at good prices. If you haven't got a similar source of materials, try overdyeing pale or neutral colors with vivid dyes. Or, if you wish to make the design as a wallhanging, experiment with bright printed cottons and/or synthetics.

SIZE
24 x 36 inches

MATERIALS
Wool fabrics in the following colors and approximate quantities
(based on 60 inch fabric):

◆ light blue tweed . . . . ¼ yard
◆ black . . . . ⅛ yard
◆ assorted colors . . . . 1¾ yards

Piece of burlap 30 x 42 inches

3¾ yards of rug-binding tape

Linen or carpet thread and large needle

Hand hook

Frame

❖

INSTRUCTIONS

1. Zigzag-stitch or overcast the edges of the backing fabric.
2. Transfer the design to the fabric using your chosen method (see pages 17–19).
3. Mount the fabric in the frame (see page 19).
4. Cut strips of fabric ½–1 inch wide, depending on its thickness.
5. Work the hooking as described on pages 20–21. The background diamonds are worked in vertical and horizontal rows, the blue rectangle in vertical rows, and the two blossoms in a circular pattern.
6. Check the rug to make sure that there are no gaps, then block it as described on page 22.
7. Bind the edges with the tape as described on pages 22–23.

KITCHEN DRESSER

❖

EMMA TENNANT

"The kitchen dresser is a constant source of ideas," says Emma Tennant. Here, a pine dresser serves as a perfect background for crockery in shades of blue, complemented by spring flowers: campanulas and tulips. It could equally well hold a bowl of fruit and a different selection of dishes. By using several shades of hand-dyed wools, the designer has achieved subtle shading on the objects, while the touch of white on the vase suggests reflected light from a nearby window.

Ideally, hand-dyed fabrics should be used for the two pitchers, vase, and flowers in this design. Green tweed has been used for the campanula stems and dark blue tweeds for the mugs.

SIZE
24 x 33½ inches

MATERIALS
Wool fabrics in the following colors and approximate quantities
(based on 60 inch fabric):

◆ shades of brown . . . . .1⅜ yards
◆ shades of cornflower blue . . . . . . .¼ yard
◆ shades of turquoise blue . . . . .¼ yard
◆ sage green tweed . . . . . . .⅛ yard
◆ shades of yellow . . . . . . .⅛ yard
◆ 2 or 3 dark blue tweeds . . . . .⅛ yard
◆ white and cream . . . . . . .scraps

Piece of burlap 30 x 39½ inches

3½ yards of rug-binding tape

Linen or carpet thread and large needle

Hand hook

Frame

❖

INSTRUCTIONS

1. Zigzag-stitch or overcast the edges of the backing fabric.
2. Transfer the design to the fabric using your chosen method (see pages 17–19).
3. Mount the fabric in the frame (see page 19).
4. Cut strips of fabric ½ inch wide.
5. Work the hooking as described on pages 20–21, following the photograph as a guide to color placement. Note that the dresser is worked almost entirely in horizontal lines, except around the flowers and leaves, where a few rows follow these curving shapes.
6. Check the rug to make sure that there are no gaps, then block it as described on page 22.
7. Bind the edges with the tape as described on pages 22–23.

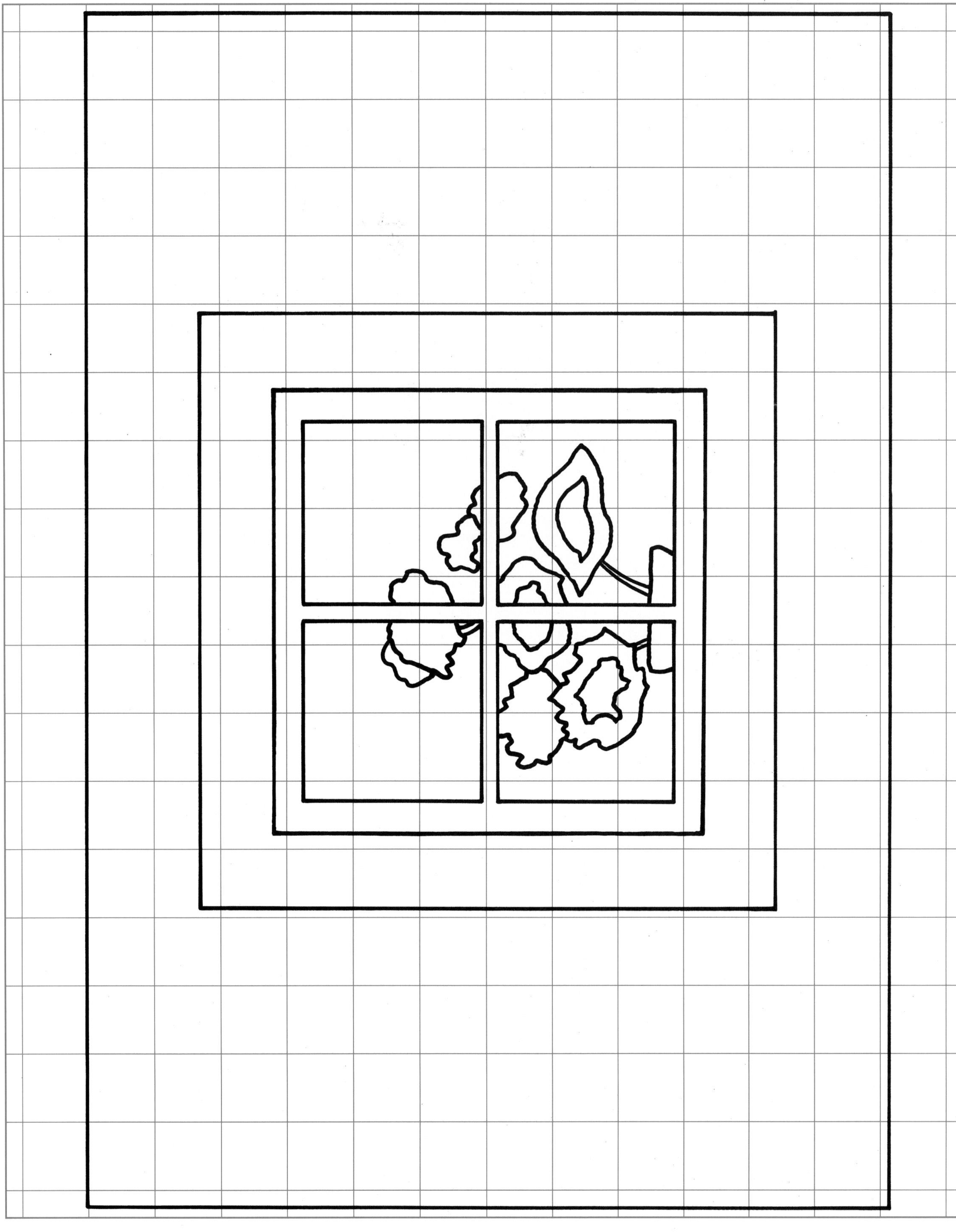

GERANIUM IN WINDOW

❖

EMMA TENNANT

This rug began as a study in geometry and contrasting textures. The
designer's eye was caught by a window in an old Scottish house,
with its simple four-pane frame deeply set into a stone recess and
surrounded by a wall of pebbledash (or harling, as this type of
rendering is called in Scotland). At first she planned to restrict the
design to rectangles, in the spirit of an Amish patchwork quilt, but
then decided that it needed a little brightening up and added the vivid
red geranium in its terracotta pot.

Doors and windows make appealing subjects for rugs; you might use a door or window from your own house as the basis for a design. Study the colors and textures carefully, and don't be afraid to embellish the feature with an imaginary plant or two if it needs something extra in order to work effectively as an image.

SIZE

24 x 34½ inches

MATERIALS

Wool fabrics in the following colors and approximate quantities
(based on 60 inch fabric):

◆ soft gold . . . . .1⅛ yards   ◆ olive green . . . . .⅛ yard
◆ gray-green . . . . .⅜ yard   ◆ forest green . . . . .⅛ yard
◆ dark gray-green . . . . . . .⅜ yard   ◆ brown . . . . .⅛ yard
◆ white . . . . .⅛ yard   ◆ terracotta . . . . .scrap
◆ red . . . . .⅛ yard

Piece of burlap 30 x 40½ inches

3½ yards of rug-binding tape

Linen or carpet thread and large needle

Hand hook

Frame

❖

INSTRUCTIONS

1. Zigzag-stitch or overcast the edges of the backing fabric.
2. Transfer the design to the fabric using your chosen method (see pages 17–19).
3. Mount the fabric in the frame (see page 19).
4. Cut strips of fabric ½ inch wide.
5. Work the hooking as described on pages 20–21, following the photograph as a guide to color placement. All the parts of the house are worked in straight lines, whereas the flowers, leaves, and interior of the room are worked in curved lines.
6. Check the rug to make sure that there are no gaps, then block it as described on page 22.
7. Bind the edges with the tape as described on pages 22–23.

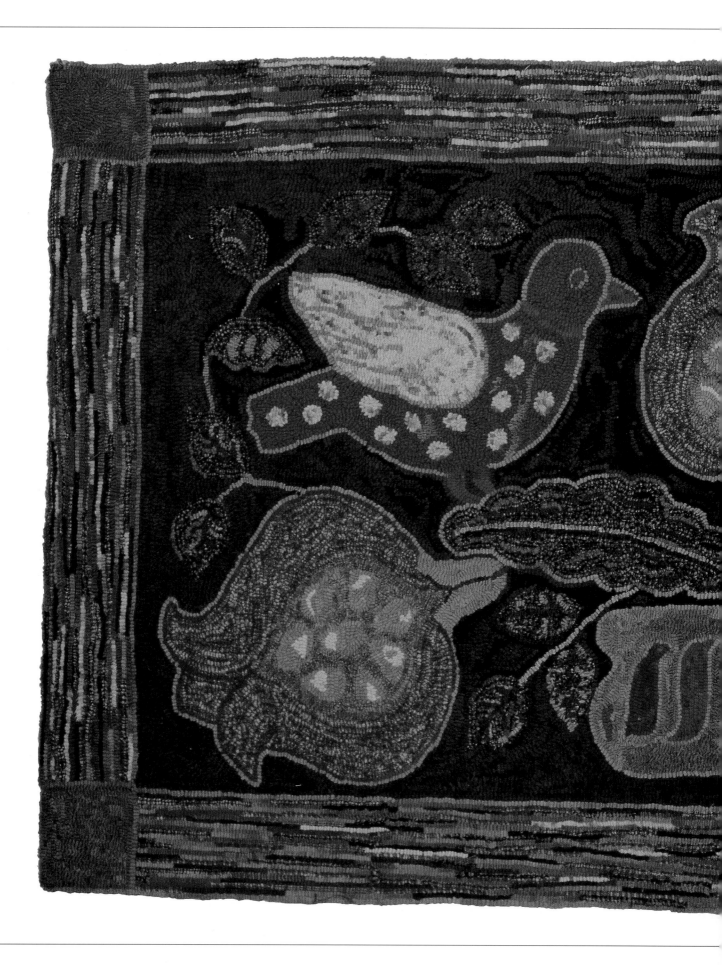

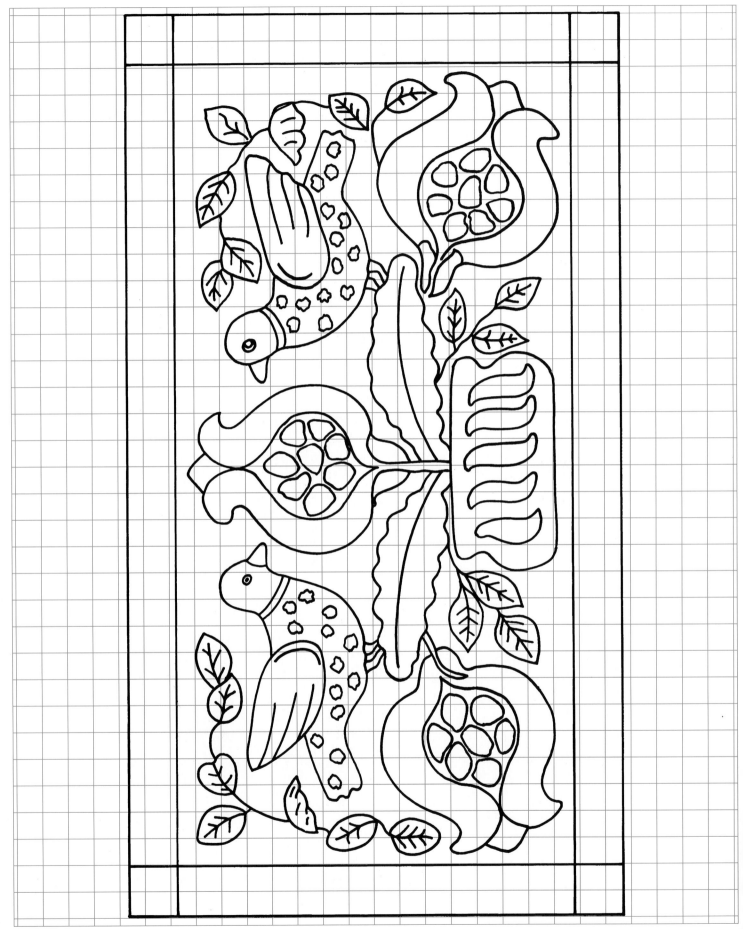

BIRDS AND POMEGRANATES

❖

POLLY MINICK
Based on a design by Edyth O'Neill

This charming rug, with its bold, flat shapes and rich, antique colors, lies unmistakably in the tradition of old American rugs. The multicolored border picks up the shades of the main motif for a lively variegated effect. Like so many of the best hooked rugs, this one relies strongly on hand-dyed fabrics for its effectiveness. However, the "antique black" of the background can be achieved by mixing an assortment of black, navy, dark brown, and very dark green strips.

SIZE
37 x 67 inches

MATERIALS
Wool fabrics in the following colors and approximate quantities
(based on 60 inch fabric):

- shades of red . . . . 1⅝ yards
- shades of gray-blue . . . 1¼ yards
- shades of gold . . . . 1¼ yards
- shades of green . . . . ¾ yard
- mixture (see above)
  for antique black . . . . . 1⅝ yards

Piece of burlap 43 x 73 inches

6⅛ yards of rug-binding tape

Linen or carpet thread and large needle

Hand hook   Frame

❖

INSTRUCTIONS

1. Zigzag-stitch or overcast the edges of the backing fabric.
2. Transfer the design to the fabric (see pages 17–19).
3. Mount the fabric in the frame (see page 19).
4. Cut strips of fabric ¼ inch wide.
5. Work the hooking as described on pages 20–21, following the photograph as a guide to color placement. Pay special attention to the use of contrasting colors for outlining the motifs. For the border, alternate strips in a random manner.
6. Check the rug to make sure that there are no gaps, then block it as described on page 22.
7. Bind the edges with the tape as described on pages 22–23.

NORWEGIAN WEDDING

❖

BETSY COLEMAN

An antique woven wallhanging depicting a wedding celebration
which Betsy found in a small hotel perched on the edge of a fjord in
Norway served as the inspiration for this rug. Old textiles—
especially those in a naïve style—can often yield promising subject
matter for hooked rugs. Look for those with simple shapes and
strong, clear colors. Appliqué quilts and pictures are good design
sources; embroidered samplers, too, often contain images that
could be adapted for rugs.

Having photographed the textile (with the owner's permission), Betsy Coleman then did some "creative copying": she projected the slide onto paper taped to a wall and traced the figures. She then enlarged them to the desired size, using graph paper, and rearranged them from their original positions, in the wallhanging's vertical format, to suit the landscape format typical of most rugs. The colors, however, correspond closely to those in the original, and although the figures are hooked in the curving rows characteristic of the craft, the background was worked in horizontal rows to suggest the woven structure of the wallhanging.

SIZE
34 x 50 inches

MATERIALS
Wool fabric in the following colors and approximate quantities
(based on 60 inch fabric):

- blue . . . . 1⅜ yards
- beige. . . . . 1 yard
- brown. . . . . 1 yard
- red-orange . . . . ¾ yard
- green. . . . . ¾ yard
- gold. . . . . ⅜ yard
- off-white . . . . ⅜ yard
- pink flesh tone . . . . ⅛ yard

Piece of burlap 40 x 56 inches

5 yards of rug-binding tape

Linen or carpet thread and large needle

Hand hook

Frame

❖

INSTRUCTIONS

1. Zigzag stitch or overcast the edges of the backing fabric.

2. Transfer the design to the fabric using your chosen method (see pages 17–19).

3. Mount the fabric in the frame (see page 19).

4. Cut strips of fabric ¼ inch wide.

5. Work the hooking as described on pages 20–21, following the photograph as a guide to color placement.

6. Check the rug to make sure that there are no gaps, then block it as described on page 22.

7. Bind the edges with the tape as described on pages 22–23.

One square = 2 inches

GOOSE IN GARDEN

❖

EMMA TENNANT

The designer of this cheerful rug admits to a certain "artistic license" in depicting a goose among the campanulas in her kitchen garden. "Poultry do not agree with flowers and vegetables," she observes; and the custom among farmers' wives of keeping chickens is one reason, she says, "why so few farms have a well-kept garden." One can certainly see, in the set of this goose's head, that she goes where she pleases.

The drystone wall makes a good background for the scene—not only because it sets off the bright, clear colors of goose, flowers, and sky but also for a practical reason: it is a good way of using up large quantities of drab brown or gray tweeds. It is important, Emma Tennant cautions, to use darker fabric to outline the stones in a drystone wall, as lighter fabrics look like mortar. If your assortment of browns and grays varies too much in tone or hue, try overdyeing them the same shade.

SIZE
24 x 34 inches

MATERIALS
Wool fabrics in the following colors and approximate quantities
(based on 60 inch fabric):

◆ shades of brown
and gray tweed ......6½ yards

◆ cream ....⅞ yard

◆ shades of blue ....½ yard

◆ dark green ....¼ yard

◆ orange ....¼ yard

Piece of burlap, 30 x 40 inches

3½ yards of rug-binding tape

Linen or carpet thread and large needle

Hand hook

Frame

❖

INSTRUCTIONS

1. Zigzag-stitch or overcast the edges of the backing fabric.
2. Transfer the design to the fabric using your chosen method (see pages 17–19).
3. Mount the fabric in the frame (see page 19).
4. Cut strips of fabric ½ inch wide.
5. Work the hooking as described on pages 20–21, following the photograph as a guide to color placement. Note that the goose is hooked following the contours of the body, whereas the wall is hooked in straight lines.
6. Check the rug to make sure that there are no gaps, then block it as described on page 22.
7. Bind the edges with tape as described on pages 22–23.

DOYLESTOWN HOUSES

❖

BETSY COLEMAN

These houses dating from Colonial times in Doylestown, Pennyslvania, have been imaginatively relocated on one street to represent the different styles of early domestic architecture still to be seen there. Because this was intended as a rug, rather than a wallhanging, Betsy Coleman decided against a blue sky: "Blues jump out at you if you're not careful." The use of three closely related shades of beige gives the sky depth and interest. She chose a dark plaid, rather than black, for the windows, so that the lighter parts of the plaid could suggest reflections.

SIZE
18 x 45 inches

MATERIALS

Wool fabrics in the following colors and approximate quantities

(based on 60 inch fabric):

- ◆ 3 shades of beige . . . . ⅝ yard
- ◆ shades of green . . . . ⅜ yard
- ◆ shades of red . . . . ¼ yard
- ◆ light brown . . . . ¼ yard
- ◆ shades of yellow . . . . ⅛ yard
- ◆ shades of blue . . . . ⅛ yard
- ◆ white . . . . ⅛ yard
- ◆ dark plaid . . . . ⅛ yard
- ◆ brown tweed . . . . ⅛ yard
- ◆ dark brown . . . . ⅛ yard
- ◆ beige-gray . . . . ⅛ yard
- ◆ mauve . . . . ⅛ yard

Piece of burlap 42 x 51 inches

4 yards of rug-binding tape

Linen or carpet thread and large needle

Hand hook   Frame

One square = 2 inches

INSTRUCTIONS

1. Zigzag-stitch or overcast the edges of the backing fabric.
2. Transfer the design to the fabric using your chosen method (see pages 17–19), making sure that the horizontal and vertical lines of the houses are aligned with the fabric grain.
3. Mount the fabric in the frame (see page 19).
4. Cut strips of fabric ³⁄₁₆ inch wide.
5. Work the hooking as described on pages 20–21, following the photograph as a guide to color placement. For the sky, hook squiggles in the darkest beige, then repeat with the lightest beige, and finally fill in the spaces with the medium tone.
6. Check the rug to make sure that there are no gaps, then block it as described on page 22.
7. Bind the edges with tape as described on pages 22–23.

BALTIMORE BEAUTIES

❖

ANN DAVIES

This elegant rug, which would look at home in a formal drawing room, is based on a style of appliqué album quilt fashionable in Baltimore, Maryland, in the nineteenth century. For an album quilt, a number of people would each contribute a single block displaying their taste and needlework skills. This rug pays tribute to that tradition with its intricate motifs, hooked in rich, muted shades of red, green, and other colors on a creamy background.

❖

For the background of this quilt Ann Davies used a twin-bed-size wool blanket which she cut up and dyed in some weak tea to give it a slightly aged look characteristic of old cotton or linen. She worked it on a special lap frame, on which the rug can be moved. If you do not have such a frame, you can work the individual blocks and sew them together, or you can overlap the edges of the blocks for about 1½–2 inches and work the hooking through both thicknesses. This can be hard on the hands but makes a better finish than a seam.

SIZE
42 x 41 inches

MATERIALS
Wool fabrics in the following colors and approximate quantities
(based on 60 inch fabric):

◆ cream-beige . . . . .2⅛ yards
◆ shades of green,
   including sage, grass,
   pale green . . . . .⅞ yard
◆ green tweed . . . . .½ yard
◆ bright red . . . . .½ yard
◆ dark red tweed . . . . .⅛ yard

◆ orange . . . . .⅛ yard
◆ dark green-brown
   tweed . . . . .⅛ yard
◆ cocoa brown . . . . .⅛ yard
◆ assorted light clear
   colors such as peach,
   yellow, mauve . . . . .scraps

Piece of burlap 48 x 47 inches,
or nine pieces, each 20 x 20 inches

5 yards of rug-binding tape

Linen or carpet thread and large needle

Hand hook

Frame

One square = 2 inches

INSTRUCTIONS

1. Zigzag-stitch or overcast the edges of the backing fabric.
2. Mark the area to be worked on the burlap, and then divide it into nine squares. Transfer each motif to the appropriate square, using your chosen method (see pages 17–19).
3. Mount the fabric in the frame (see page 19).
4. Cut strips of fabric ¼ inch wide.
5. Work the hooking as described on pages 20–21, following the photograph as a guide to color placement.
6. Check the rug to make sure that there are no gaps, then block it as described on page 22.
7. Bind the edges with the tape as described on pages 22–23.

Detail of central motif

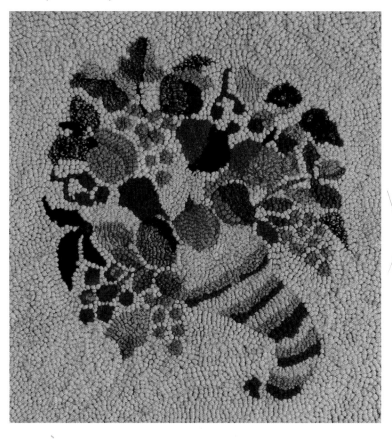

FLOWER SQUARES

❖

CAROLE RENNISON AND SUE SHEARS

For this fresh floral design the traditional hooking technique has
been worked with rug yarn, mainly in shades of blue, pink, and burgundy.
Lines of mock blanket stitch provide a framework for the motifs.

Enlarge each square to 8 inches

The yarn used for this rug is a two-ply rug yarn, 80 percent wool and 20 percent synthetic fiber, which the designers obtain as waste yarn from a carpet manufacturer and which is classifed "2/47." If you cannot obtain this yarn, a lightweight rya yarn is an acceptable substitute.

SIZE
32 x 48 inches

MATERIALS
Rug yarn (see above) in the following colors
and approximate quantities:

◆ cream . . . . .27 ounces
◆ green . . . . .10 ounces
◆ rose pink . . . . .15 ounces
◆ blue . . . . .4 ounces
◆ ice blue . . . . .14 ounces
◆ white . . . . .4 ounces
◆ charcoal . . . . .14 ounces
◆ burgundy . . . . .3 ounces

Piece of 12-oz burlap 38 x 54 inches

4¾ yards of rug-binding tape

Hand hook

Frame

❖

INSTRUCTIONS

1. Zigzag-stitch or overcast the edges of the backing fabric.

2. Mark the finished size of the rug on the burlap, then divide this area into twenty-four 8-inch squares. Enlarge the motifs as indicated (opposite) and transfer them to the fabric (see pages 17–19), reversing some as shown in the photograph.

3. Mount the fabric in the frame (see page 19).

4. Work the hooking as described on pages 20–21, following the photograph as a guide to color placement. The charcoal gray lines of the grid which look like blanket stitch are simply loops worked in short straight lines.

5. Check the rug to make sure that there are no gaps, then block it as described on page 22.

6. Bind the edges with the tape as described on pages 22–23.

SOUVENIR

❖

JUJU VAIL

This vivid evocation of Canada was designed for the office of the
cultural attaché to the Canadian High Commission in London.
Its images include a maple leaf, symbol of Canada, and various motifs
used in the beadwork souvenirs produced by native Canadians for
the tourist trade—a few pieces of actual beadwork have been applied
near the top edge above some fanciful shapes that suggest
the nation's European heritage.

A great variety of materials were used for this wallhanging: cottons, wools, synthetics, plastics, and silks. Some of the loops were left uncut, some sheared for a velvety texture. In most places, two different-colored strips were hooked together.

SIZE
39½ x 53½ inches

MATERIALS
An assortment of fabrics of different types, in the following colors and approximate quantities (based on 60 inch fabric):

- ◆ cherry red . . . . ¾ yard
- ◆ dark red . . . . ⅝ yard
- ◆ deep pink . . . . ⅝ yard
- ◆ orange . . . . ½ yard
- ◆ pink . . . . ⅜ yard
- ◆ black . . . . ½ yard
- ◆ medium brown . . . . ⅜ yard
- ◆ bright gold . . . . ⅜ yard
- ◆ old gold . . . . ¼ yard
- ◆ yellow . . . . ¼ yard
- ◆ pale yellow . . . . ¼ yard
- ◆ white . . . . ¼ yard
- ◆ dark blue . . . . ¼ yard
- ◆ deep lilac . . . . ¼ yard
- ◆ pale lilac . . . . ¼ yard
- ◆ turquoise . . . . ⅛ yard

Four small beadwork motifs (optional)

Piece of burlap 46 x 60 inches

5½ yards of rug-binding tape

Linen or carpet thread and large needle

Hand hook

Frame

❖

INSTRUCTIONS

1. Zigzag-stitch or overcast the edges of the backing fabric.

2. Transfer the design to the fabric (see pages 17–19).

3. Mount the fabric in the frame (see page 19).

4. Cut strips of fabric ⅜–1¼ inches wide.

5. Work the hooking as described on pages 20–21, following the photograph as a guide to color. Work the writing and other fine black lines before the surrounding area. The rows to either side of these lines should be worked in a single color and left uncut for a well-defined effect.

6. Check the rug to make sure that there are no gaps, then block it as described on page 22.

7. Bind the edges with tape as described on pages 22–23.

FLORAL STAINED GLASS

❖

ANN DAVIES

With its bright colors outlined in black, this rug evokes the
stained glass of Louis Comfort Tiffany and the graceful Art Nouveau
style of the late 1800s.

The woolen fabrics used for the hooking were all hand dyed by the designer. Because hand dyeing tends to produce tonal variations, she had to cut the strips selectively to obtain the pure colors characteristic of stained glass. Fabric amounts are generous, to allow for this; you can save unused scraps for your next project.

SIZE
Diameter: 37 inches

MATERIALS
Wool fabric in the following colors and approximate quantities
(based on 60 inch fabric):

◆ light orange . . . . ⅜ yard   ◆ dark green . . . . ⅛ yard
◆ black . . . . ¼ yard   ◆ light turquoise . . . . ⅛ yard
◆ light green . . . . ¼ yard   ◆ dark blue . . . . ⅛ yard
◆ medium yellow . . . . ¼ yard   ◆ medium blue . . . . ⅛ yard
◆ yellow-orange . . . . ¼ yard   ◆ light green . . . . ⅛ yard
◆ lilac . . . . ¼ yard   ◆ pink . . . . ⅛ yard
◆ purple . . . . ⅛ yard   ◆ purple-gray . . . . ⅛ yard
◆ turquoise . . . . ⅛ yard   ◆ yellow-gray . . . . ⅛ yard
◆ pale blue . . . . ⅛ yard   ◆ lilac-gray . . . . ⅛ yard
◆ yellow . . . . ⅛ yard   ◆ pale lilac . . . . ⅛ yard

Piece of fine burlap 43 inches square

5 yards of rug-binding tape

Linen or carpet thread and large needle

Hand hook   Frame

❖

INSTRUCTIONS

1. Zigzag-stitch or overcast the edges of the backing fabric.
2. Transfer the design to the fabric (see pages 17–19).
3. Mount the fabric in the frame (see page 19).
4. Cut strips of fabric ¼ inch wide.
5. Work the hooking as described on pages 20–21. Begin with the black outlines, making these loops slightly higher than the others will be, so that they will not get lost. Use the photograph as a guide to color placement. Work the larger flowers and the stems first, to get those colors in place, then go on to fill in the other colors. Don't worry about duplicating the photograph exactly—an impossible goal; your shades will be different, in any case.
6. Check the rug to make sure that there are no gaps, then block it as described on page 22.
7. Bind the edges with the tape as described on pages 22–23.

One square = 2 inches

One square = 2 inches

FATHER CHRISTMAS

❖

POLLY MINICK

To welcome guests at Christmas time, this festive rug, featuring an
old-style version of Santa bearing a tree and a bag full of presents,
is ideal. Place it in the hallway to mark the start of the holidays.

This design exemplifies Polly Minick's love of strong yet muted colors. If your fabrics are too bright, experiment with dyes to tone them down a little, so that your rug, too, will look as though it's been in the family for several generations.

SIZE
36 x 36 inches

MATERIALS
Wool fabrics in the following colors and approximate quantities
(based on 60 inch fabric):

- gold-beige . . . . .1⅝ yards
- red and green
  plaid . . . . .¾ yard
- red . . . . .½ yard
- jade green . . . . .½ yard
- brown . . . . .⅛ yard
- white . . . . .⅛ yard
- dark green . . . . .⅛ yard
- green and brown
  tweed . . . . .scrap
- black . . . . .scrap
- pink flesh color . . . . .scrap

Piece of burlap 42 x 42 inches

4¼ yards of rug-binding tape

Linen or carpet thread and large needle

Hand hook

Frame

❖

INSTRUCTIONS

1. Zigzag-stitch or overcast the edges of the backing fabic.
2. Transfer the design to the fabric using your chosen method (see pages 17–19).
3. Mount the fabric in the frame (see page 19).
4. Cut strips of fabric ¼ inch wide.
5. Work the hooking as described on pages 20–21, following the photograph as a guide to color placement.
6. Check the rug to make sure that there are no gaps, then block it as described on page 22.
7. Bind the edges with the tape as described on pages 22–23.

THE RUG MAKERS

Barbara Carroll lives in the historic old town of Ligonier, Pennsylvania, where she and her husband offer bed and breakfast in their picturesque stone cottage, the Woolley Fox. Realizing that this was the perfect setting for sharing her enthusiasm for rug hooking, she started, in 1994, a spring workshop. Over five days, students have the opportunity to develop their skills in primitive rug hooking, under the guidance of well-known teachers of this style. Barbara's own work shows a flair for whimsy and, especially, for coloring. *The Woolley Fox, 61 Old Lincoln Highway, East Ligonier, PA 15658. Tel. 412 238 3004.*

Betsy Coleman's love of folk art traditions is vividly reflected in the rugs she has been hooking for the past twenty-five years. Most of them have been inspired by events in her own life, in Doylestown, Pennsylvania, and on trips abroad. As a teacher of the craft, she encourages her students to create their own designs and not be inhibited by doubts about their drawing ability. While acknowledging that artistic training is a "plus," she maintains that even without it, by using our natural talents "we grow in appreciation of design and color and have a wonderful time in the process."

Ann Davies first became interested in rag rugs while studying textiles at Goldsmiths' College, London, in the 1960s. Since then she has pursued a busy career as rug maker, teacher, and writer of books on the subject. Her rugs—which display a love of pattern and the imaginative use of materials—have been featured in many exhibitions, including a one-woman show at the Royal Festival Hall, London, in 1986, and have been purchased by private collectors in Britain, the United States, and Italy. She has demonstrated the craft of rug hooking on television and has conducted many weekend and day courses in it. She is available for commissions. *1 Wingrad House, Jubilee Street, London E1 3BJ, U.K. Tel. 0171 790 1093.*

Joan Dennis hooks rugs "for the sheer pleasure of it." Although she has had no formal art training, she has been interested in art for "as long as I can remember" and enjoys painting, as well as rug making. Her first rugs were in a relatively formal style, using fine strips of fabric, but this style did not capture her imagination, and it was only in 1991, when she began to hook in a more primitive style, that she took up the craft with enthusiasm. Since then she has designed and made more than thirty-five hooked rugs and other items. *P.O. Box 1315, Kennebunkport, ME 04046-1315. Tel. 207 967 3262.*

Happy and Steve DiFranza have been producing hooked rugs since 1968. Although both members of this husband-and-wife team have studied art, Steve now does the actual designing for their business, while Happy does "everything else"—interpreting the designs in fabric and running the business, while also teaching classes and workshops in hooking. The DiFranzas consciously avoid traditional-style floral designs, which are abundant in the market, concentrating instead on animals and themes from children's literature. Their rugs have been featured in a number of exhibitions and publications. *DiFranza Designs, 25 Bow Street, North Reading, MA 01864. Tel. 508 664 2034.*

Liz Kitching studied textile design at the Cumbria College of Art and Design. In 1980 she moved to London, where she worked initially as a freelance fabric designer. Two years later she established a workshop, in which she produced hand-tufted rugs, receiving many important commissions from architects and interior designers. Today she has returned to Cumbria and now designs and makes rag rugs and holds occasional workshops in the craft. She encourages her students to experiment freely with materials and methods, avoiding the notion that there is a single "right" way to work. *Hill Cottage, Walton, Brampton, Cumbria CA8 2EA, U.K. Tel. 01697 741539.*

Polly Minick first learned the hooking craft in order to furnish her Michigan home with the kind of traditional rugs suitable for it. Failing to find what she was looking for in commercially available designs, she started designing her own. With the help of an art student, she refined her style, while retaining its childlike simplicity. The primitive effect is enhanced by her use of recycled materials, which she overdyes in warm, muted colors. Polly's rugs have been sold to galleries in Houston and New York, where she had an exhibition of her work in 1995. *3111 Dale View Drive, Ann Arbor, MI 48105. Tel. 313 995 5361.*

Carole Rennison and Sue Shears In 1993 Sue Shears, a Canadian, and Carole Rennison, an Englishwoman, joined forces to create the company Hooked by Design, based in the

Yorkshire Dales, which produces hooked rug and cushion kits. While incorporating elements of traditional English design, North American folk art imagery, and oriental rug styles, their work has a fresh, modern look, in keeping with contemporary tastes. The designs are worked in yarn, which is provided with the kits, thus making the projects especially approachable by beginners. Carole and Sue have demonstrated the craft at exhibitions and have recently begun offering a series of workshops. *Weavers Cottage, 18 Main Street, Bradley, near Keighley, West Yorkshire BD20 9DG, U.K. Tel. 01535 636934.*

Olga Rothschild's rugs have been displayed at many exhibitions, including a one-woman show at the Adirondack Lakes Center for the Arts in 1991, and have appeared in several publications, notably *Rug Hooking* magazine. A liberal arts graduate and M.A. (Sarah Lawrence College), Olga also studied art, chiefly sculpture and printmaking—her father's profession. She began hooking rugs in the mid-1980s. She cuts the wool fabric by hand and hooks it into a linen backing, which she finds pleasanter to work with than burlap and which, with its regular weave, lends itself to the geometric designs she favors. She is available for commissions. *105 Standish Street, Duxbury, MA 02332.*

Beth Sekerka says that the greatest compliment anyone can pay one of her rugs is to say that it looks like an antique. Her work is emphatically in the primitive style, with its simple, almost childlike shapes and cheerful disregard of perspective. When Beth took up rug hooking, in 1983, she was delighted to discover how simple and relaxing it is. Previously an English teacher, she changed careers after her family moved to Michigan in 1988, when she began teaching rug hooking, and then established her own business, Hooked on Rugs. With the help of her husband, Karl, who designs many of the rugs, she offers a range of kits to a growing clientele. *Hooked on Rugs, 44492 Midway Drive, Novi, MI 48375. Tel. 810 344 4367.*

Beth Snyder describes herself as a "life-long crafter," having applied her talents to stenciling, quilting, and other decorative arts at various times. She discovered rug hooking shortly after attending college (where she studied sociology and criminal justice), and she has now turned this pastime into a business. She and her husband, Tom, also deal in antiques, and many of her rug designs are inspired by antique pieces. Others draw their subject matter from the countryside around their home in Connecticut. *11 Fairwood Road, Bethany, CT 06524.*

Emma Tennant spent her childhood in Derbyshire, then read history at Oxford. She now lives in the Scottish Border country, where she and her husband raise cattle and sheep. These and other resident animals figure prominently in her hooked rugs, which she has been making for the past fifteen years. Flowers are another favorite subject—especially for her watercolors; an exhibition of these was held in New York in 1994. Her painting and rug hooking complement and influence each other, both exemplifying her preference for images that are "bold, simple and unfussy." Her rugs are marketed under the name Hermitage Rugs. *Shaws, Newcastleton, Roxburghshire TD9 0SH, U.K.*

Juju Vail was born in Canada and has lived in Britain since 1991. She studied art at the Collège Lasalle, Montreal, and St. Martin's College of Art and Design in London, from which she received an M.A. in 1994. In both countries she has made a name for herself as a textile artist—first with knitwear and more recently with hooked rugs. She has received numerous awards for her work and she is available for commissions. *6 Alconbury, London E5 8RH, U.K. Tel. 0181 806 7804.*

❖ HOOKED RUG SUPPLIES ❖

Hooks for rug making can be obtained from needlecraft stores, as can burlap, rug-binding tape, and other basic materials and equipment. Artist's stretchers, tracing paper, and graph paper are available from art supply stores. Your local Yellow Pages should list useful retailers for this craft.

For more specialized equipment, including rug-making frames, and for suppliers of suitable fabrics and dyes, as well as the names and addresses of teachers and designers, consult *Rug Hooking Magazine*, P.O. Box 15760, Cameron and Kelker Streets, Harrisburg, PA 17105. Tel. 717 234 5091.

INDEX

❖